St.
Peter's
B-LIST

"This book is a treasure!"

James Martin, S.J.
Author of *My Life with the Saints*

"A lush and generous feast of saint-inspired poems that both invite and challenge. A lovely collection!"

Christine Valters Paintner
Author of *Eyes of the Heart*

"This lovely new anthology offers us true spiritual food, perfect for lectio divina. *St. Peter's B-list* proves that poems can indeed be prayers."

Paula Huston
Author of *Simplifying the Soul*

St. Peter's B-List

Contemporary Poems Inspired by the Saints

edited by

Mary Ann B. Miller

ave maria press AmP notre dame, indiana

The title of this book, *St. Peter's B-list*, is from the poem of the same name by Jake Oresick and is used with his permission.

Acknowledgments begin on page 203, which is a continuation of this copyright page.

Founded in 1865, Ave Maria Press is a ministry of the United States Province of Holy Cross.

www.avemariapress.com

Paperback ISBN-13 978-1-59471-474-0

E-book ISBN-13 978-1-59471-475-7

Cover image © Millennium Images / SuperStock.

Cover and text design by Andy Wagoner.

Printed and bound in the United States of America.

for Bob and Caroline

Contents

II. Faith and Worship

III. Sickness and Death

Foreword

In the final week of his sixteenth-century handbook *Spiritual Exercises*, St. Ignatius asked the person making a retreat to contemplate created things as a way of seeing how God shares himself and his gifts with the world. Ignatius asked that the retreatant "look how God dwells in creatures, in the elements, giving them being, in the plants vegetating, in the animals feeling, in men giving them to understand; and so in me, giving me being, animating me, giving me sensation and making me understand; likewise making a temple of me, being created to the likeness and image of His Divine Majesty."

Roman Catholic theologian David Tracy would see in such a contemplation an example of the analogical imagination, that is, the tendency of painters, writers, and theologians to view and represent the world as a metaphor of the Holy One. As fiction writer Flannery O'Connor put it, the Catholic artist "penetrates the concrete world in order to find at its depths the image of its source, the image of ultimate reality."

Swedish journalist Runar Eldebo contrasted that analogical imagination with a Protestant imagination, which he felt was dialectic. "According to the Protestant imagination, Karl Barth for example, God is hidden everywhere but found only in the revelation of Jesus Christ. Therefore . . . Protestants are never at home on the earth, they are pilgrims on their way."

Whether written by a Catholic or not, the 106 fascinating poems in *St. Peter's B-list* are all representations of an analogical imagination that finds the immanence of God in earthly things.

A lovely example of the anthology's subtitle, *Contemporary Poems Inspired by the Saints*, is Angela Alaimo O'Donnell's "Waiting for Ecstasy." In it O'Donnell imagines St. Thérèse of Lisieux prostrate on a French chapel floor in a state of overpowering piety and alternates the stanzas with glimpses of herself handling laundry chores as she yearns for the gift of the ecstatic saint's deep intimacy with God. We are all that narrator.

Also consider the stunning "In Praise of Single Mothers" by Kate Daniels. A mother hoping to work on a poem one night is interrupted by her almost four-year-old son. She's reminded of "self-sacrificing saints" such as St. Zita and St. Paula as she gets him to bed; then as she returns to her poem again she hears the wailing of her newborn daughter and leaves her unfinished work to breast-feed the infant. And we have a feminine image of God as "she drains me and I do not / even care, holding her there / in the time-stopped, milky darkness," recognizing "That I love her more, / much more, than poetry."

Look, too, at Paul Mariani's "Manhattan." Except for a glancing mention of St. Thomas Aquinas's thoughts on ends and means, there are no references to saints or religion. There is simply a rhyming, seemingly autobiographical narrative of a wild night in Hempstead, Long Island, when after five beers and five Manhattans the poet defended his Manhattan College jacket by throttling a sneering man outside the bar. "And in two minutes it's over, & through a blur / of cheers I'm downing five Manhattans more." Because Mariani alerted us earlier to a college ethics test the next morning, we become convinced that there will be remorse and a penance for the sodden recklessness he was prey to. And we get it in a foolish accident that he's scarred by even now.

I mention those fine poems only to sample the poignance, vividness, and variety of Mary Ann B. Miller's collection. As with Jake Oresick's funny final poem, which the editor chose for the book's title, there's a purgatorial aspect to most of the offerings, the already-but-not-yet quality of our enjoyment of the kingdom of God. And each reminds us of the heartening final claims of "The Angelus": "The Word was made flesh. And dwelt among us."

Ron Hansen

Editor's Acknowledgments

Special thanks to Gina Scalise, librarian at Poets House in New York City, whose help with finding collections of poems went far beyond the service of a library that is not a research library; to Elizabeth Willse, Poets House volunteer and master's student in library and information science at the Pratt Institute, for her enthusiastic support during my days in the reading room of Poets House; to Joan Reamer, reference librarian at Caldwell College's Jennings Library in Caldwell, New Jersey, for her numerous and always gracious efforts in helping me locate many of these poets' collections through interlibrary loan; to Brianna Ongsiako, Jennings Library volunteer and master's student in library and information science at Rutgers, for her aid in research for the marketing proposal; to poet Diane Lockward for encouraging me to conduct an Internet "call" for poems to the Yahoo! group Creative Writers Opportunities, through which I have been introduced to many of the poets in this book; to Sister Elizabeth Michael Boyle, O.P., professor emerita of English at Caldwell College, for her valuable advice when preparing the book proposal to send to publishers; to poet Alan Berecka, reference librarian at Del Mar College in Corpus Christi, Texas, for his careful research and attentive composition of the saints' biographies in the back of this book; to poet Judith Valente, on-air correspondent for the national PBS-TV program *Religion and Ethics NewsWeekly*, whose enthusiasm about the concept of this book and whose knowledge and undaunted direction led to its finding a publisher; to poet Jake Oresick for his imagination and humor in the title of his poem and for granting permission to use it as the title of this book; and finally to *all* of the poets for their responsiveness and dedication to this project. By far, the most joy from work on this book has come, not only from discovering their poems, but also from establishing enduring personal interaction with them that continues to give me great hope for the future of poetry.

Introduction

In the mid-1960s, southern Catholic fiction writer Flannery O'Connor attempted to define the term "Catholic novelist" in her essay "Catholic Novelists and Their Readers": "The Catholic novelist doesn't have to be a saint; he doesn't even have to be a Catholic; he does, unfortunately, have to be a novelist." It is with this same understanding and in this same spirit that I call the poems that follow Catholic poems and their authors Catholic poets. I am making no judgment upon whether the author is a practicing Catholic, only that the content of these poems contains a basic underlying assumption that is essentially Catholic: the voices in these poems reflect belief in and hope for, often in spite of themselves, eventual union with God.

When O'Connor expresses misgivings at the difficult task of being a true "novelist," she opens up the need for discussing what she means by "novelist." She maintains with fiction, as I do here with poetry, an incarnative view of art. Christ's humanity validates the natural world as wholly able to reveal to us the presence of the divinity within it. This divine presence in the human world makes itself known over and over again at any point in history, first through Christ, but later whenever God's grace is manifest through human experience. A correspondence exists between the human and divine realms, such that no writer can lead us to divine Truth without first characterizing human speech and action in a believable way.

In her essay "Novelist and Believer," O'Connor explains the quality that makes human character believable by appropriating Aristotle's definition of a tragic hero for her Christian aesthetic: "The serious writer has always taken the flaw in human nature for his starting point, usually the flaw in an otherwise admirable character. Drama usually bases itself on the bedrock of original sin, whether the writer thinks in theological terms or not." For a work of art, be it a novel, drama, or poem, to be a "good" work does not mean that the characters are drawn to be morally good but that their speech and actions follow the laws of probability in the human, or natural, world. Good works of literature have intrinsic artistic merit because they avoid sentimentality—the depiction of moral innocence at the expense of qualities of character that remind us of our need for redemption. Catholic poems, as well as Catholic novels, remind us of our need for Christ, regardless of whether the poets themselves explicitly profess this concept in their poems.

To remind readers of the continually repeated presence of the divine in the human world, I have chosen poems that are not historical poems. That is, the speakers of these poems are not the saints themselves, speaking about incidents in their lives from distant time periods, but they are contemporary voices speaking from within some very contemporary dramatic situations. The great number of these figures and the wide variety of social, regional, and occupational circumstances from which they speak is reminiscent of the "communion of saints" and the litany that springs from trying to convey the individuality of these people who lived in particular times and places in the form of a necessarily limited list.

Indeed, any attempt to convey the uniqueness of the speakers in these poems turns into a litany itself: a mother trying to get her newborn to fall asleep at 3:00 a.m., a man returning to a depressed coal town in western Pennsylvania after abandoning it, a factory worker playing a mean-spirited prank on a coworker, a Native American child experiencing the pains of assimilation in a Catholic school, an older brother concerned about the kind of marriage his younger sister might make, a burn victim's compassion for a small child with whom he shares a hospital room, a woman holding the hand of her dying mother, a Catholic woman whose marriage to a Jewish man causes her father's rejection, a woman who is estranged from her mother because of her conversion to Catholicism, a woman doing laundry, a homeless woman, a woman who has rediscovered the joys of cycling after twenty years, deer hunters, a jogger, a yogi, an alcoholic, a disillusioned nurse whose back goes out from lifting so many bodies, a friend of a gay person who died young, a friend of a woman who attempted suicide, a townsperson reflecting on a man who left the priesthood, an unemployed woman sending out résumés, a patron of a food pantry who finds money on the floor, a patron of a beauty salon, pilgrims visiting the incorrupt remains of saints' bodies, art lovers contemplating a worship space or visual art, a classical music DJ dying of cancer, a flood victim who receives FEMA money for a destroyed home, a college student who drank too much the night before an exam, a young man trying to meet a woman in a bar, among others. These voices are those of mothers about children, fathers about children, daughters about mothers, daughters about fathers, sons about fathers, sons about mothers, husbands about wives, wives about husbands, sisters about brothers, brothers about sisters, singles, neighbors about neighbors, friends about friends, and adults looking back on their childhood faith.

Once immersed in the research of Victorian poetry, I have grown quite accustomed to poetic methods of deflecting charges of sentimentality in literature, and so in working on this collection, I have continually found Robert Browning's words to his friend Milsand in the 1863 dedication to *Sordello* to serve my aim well. In this brief epistle, Browning downplays the importance of the historical background in which he imbeds his speakers' words, emphasizing that his "stress lay on the incidents in the development of a soul: little else is worth study." As in Browning's poems, these speakers are souls in process, not souls at rest or peace with their spiritual states. These speakers do not address the saint directly, as if in prayer. They remember the saint in the midst of daily activity while demonstrating varying degrees of belief in or practice of the Catholic faith. Some of them seem to believe in the saint despite a pervasive sense of doubt about religious faith in general. For others, remembering a saint seems to be the last vestige of any formal practice of Catholicism in their lives. Still others identify very personally and very intimately with the saint. Many show a profound sense of humor about the reality of the saint and sainthood that is a strong indicator of a higher level of security in their beliefs than they might openly profess.

Regardless of their level of identification with the saint, all the speakers make readers think about their own relationship to sainthood and ultimately the possibility of their own union with God, despite a prevailing sense of self-doubt about being saints themselves. Most of us, I think, imagine we would be on St. Peter's B-list, invited to the dimly-lit bar after space is allocated for the canonized in the well-lit banquet hall. Nonetheless, belief that the saints have essentially "made it to heaven" makes them attractive figures, showing the relevancy of faith in the saints to contemporary life, and while these poems are not prayers themselves, they give credence to the concept of seeking intercession in the midst of many hardships. These poems show us spiritual movement within the souls of their speakers, not stasis. In the spirit of Browning, little else is worth reading.

I.

Family and Friends

Poor Banished Children of Eve

Martha Silano

I believe in the dish in the sink
not bickering about the dish in the sink
though I believe the creator

of the mess in the living room
cleans up the mess in the living room
sucks up cracker pizza potpie peanut popcorn

and I believe in the earth which also ends up on the rug
which must also be vacuumed up as I acknowledge
our blessings running water not teeming with toxins

and even though this might sound like nagging
especially in the face of dying and of burial
and of purgatory and of hell especially when

I could be instead of asking could you please
wipe up the olive juice that little pile of parsley
wailing and moaning at your wake

or maybe just sitting there stunned where beside me
sitteth the six year old and the 19 month old who most definitely
wouldn't get the dying concept though maybe the son

from thence being the owner of two dozen dead ladybugs
And I believe in the holy in the hole in the toe
of his feet-in pajamas *Mama look how much I grew*

in just one night! His reminder I own a sewing kit
and also all the holy saints (especially the martyrs)
the resurrection of peace-sign pasta three nights running

and the father of course thy will be done
though in fact a whole lot doesn't get done
like fixing the cracked windows re-upping prescriptions

or dusting let's not forget dusting hallowed be the trip
to Safeway for lettuce yogurt our daily beer
and lead us away from bitching about picking up

the hallowed son from the bus-stop
lead us away from resenting the filing
the trips to the curb to the bank

lead us away from martyrdom
(though did we mention we love the saints)
lead us away from the temptation to chuck it all flee

to Thetis Island and glory be to dishwashing liquid
and the sponge glory to the microwave and Mr. Coffee
for the world and all its Huggies all its wet wipes

glory be and have mercy and save us from the pot
of boiling water from the fires otherwise known
as letting the smoke-alarm battery go dead

to thee do we cry poor banished children of Eve
poor ants at the mercy of unforeseen disaster
poor praying mantises stuck in our plastic cages

poor and thankless a valley of tears
though actually a giant crevasse
grant us eternal grant us merciful
o clement o loving o sweet

Miracle Blanket

Erika Meitner

My mother calls it
that straitjacket.
Do you still put
the baby to sleep
in that straitjacket?
she asks, and I say
Mom, you mean
the miracle blanket?
and she says *yes,*
the straitjacket,
and I have to
admit she's right,
that it looks
like a straitjacket
for babies, especially
in the "natural" color
which resembles a tortilla
so when he's wrapped
the baby seems like a
burrito with a head,
and some nights
the straitjacket
helps him sleep, but
some nights
it does not
though we follow
step-by-step
instructions
and we shush and
swing the baby
wrapped tight

in his straitjacket,
but he screams and
won't go down,
which is what we
call sleep now—
going down, as if he's
drowning in his
straitjacket at 3 a.m.
in our bedroom
and we want him
to drown—we'll do
anything to make him
go down, even pray.
Nicholas of Tolentino,
the patron saint
of babies, is said
to have resurrected
over 100 dead children,
including several
who had drowned
together. He always
told those he helped
to *say nothing of this*.
Holy innocence, my son
in his miracle blanket
is sleeping. O faithful
and glorious martyr,
say nothing of this.

In Praise of Single Mothers

acknowledging C. S.

Kate Daniels

That I have closed myself into my study at 8:45 p.m. on this
   Thursday evening in early October,
the paper before me, the word processor whirring for revisions,
   the coffee in its thick blue mug
fragrancing this small space beside the washing machine
which, too, whirs companionably (fifth time today).

That my chores are done, my children sleeping, and I have just
   begun to make relation with words again,
a sweet tinkly string of them tumbling lightly, back of my teeth,
about to erupt, when

The magisterial Peter Augustus, forty-five months on the planet
   today,
only recently weaned of his bedtime bottle,
the one with black hair and big ears
whose eyes squint suspiciously at every encounter,
it was he, intelligent and terrifying, who took the key
to the minivan and started it up, and drove it in reverse
one hundred yards down the boulevard, trying to stop it
with his hands pressed to the roof, ignorant
of steering, grim-lipped and dry-eyed, stalling out,
thank God, on the lip of a curb, placed there, obviously,
for just that reason. He, he is the one
who pushes through the bifold doors of my makeshift study
and holds forth his sippy cup with furious civility.

That I love his fierce will, his inability to compromise,
his sweet, sleek ass, the thumb in his mouth, the pale skin
   tightened

over the harp of his ribs. That his ear
is a spiral of unspeakable wonderment, a pinkish
cornucopia lined with hair, buttered with gold—
and down deep, last week, the black bean blocking the outer canal.

That I give thanks for his uniqueness in the universe
and fill his cup and chat quietly,
and pick him up in his Tiger t-shirt,
his long legs wrapped around my waist,
sucked thumb sickeningly scented,
mouth working busily at the plastic cover of his drinking cup.

That I carry him back upstairs, fifty-four pounds
straining my back, my neck tense, quadriceps pulling manfully,
and lay him down in his bed and lean into him again and again,
finally inhaling one last time, and tiptoe out, taking his beloved
    odor
with me on my fingertips and cheeks.

That I enclose myself once more in the laundry room/study,
    pondering briefly
the nature of discipline, remembering the self-sacrificing saints,
    especially
        St. Zita, lifelong servant, patroness of washerwomen,
        charladies, housekeepers, cooks, and St. Paula, widowed
        at thirty-three with five small children, renowned for her
        "excessive" self-mortification.
I try to be like St. Theresa of Lisieux, that exquisite
Little Flower, not mystic at all, living her simple life, finding
sainthood and sanity in the daily round of cleaning up and bringing
    order.

That I am not a saint, my days are marked by bitten lips and cutoff,
    angry words, my voice
rising impatiently with creatures too undeveloped to understand
those wings inside me, rising up wildly in protest of one more
    interruption.

That the Hail Mary calms me with its lovely images, its soothing rhythms,
its praise for women, I say it like a mantra.

That I say three, then four, then close the study door again, shutting myself
once more into solitude.

That I whisk my mind into a stiff froth of egg white–like consistency and
lower myself into it as a mother and arise, rinsed into a poet, baptized
back into words.

That something flows. The liquid of language, that liquor,
the familiar warmth, the watch melting off my arm, body
disappearing into timeless space: a sound, a rhythm, an urge
to follow. That I am flying here, and floating there, and rising
and writing . . .

Like a snake in unfamiliar territory, advancing warily, but slowly gaining in confidence
and volume, a sound is born.

That she wails, she wails, she wails.

That I arise and go to her automatically.

That this one, at least, is quiet, can't talk, and fits
into one arm's crook, tightly bound inside a blanket,
I am thankful, and so race to retrieve her.
That the breasts turn on in concert, predictable
as a percolator on automatic timer, the milk
warming and rising, the breasts suddenly stuffed
sausages, uncomfortable and embarrassing.

That I love my milk, my mother's milk,
thin and sweet, yellow and oily,

and she does, too, wailing now
at a volume that threatens the sleep of the others.
That I lift her up hastily with one hand,
the other ripping at the clever closing
of the nursing bra, the pads already soaked through
and dropping to the floor with a sodden thunk.

That she clamps on with a moan, and wrenches
my nipple with her toothless, bone-hard gums,
reproaching me for my tardiness.
That my last line written downstairs—was it
a line? an entire line? maybe just an image, fleeting but brilliant—
that last hard-earned line (or whatever it was) must still be blink-
    ing behind
the cursor, mustn't it? Unless
I forgot to save it again.

That the milk is flowing now,
the endorphins surging through my head and torso,
even the pads of my feet feel good,
we tumble backward, she and I, onto the futon
her father and I conceived her on.
That I think about that for awhile, body swelling
and pulsing in various locations.
Whatever that line was, I can't
worry about it now, the machine
has it, surely. Entirely, I trust
technology, though I'm milk
and heat, white softness and the smell
her mouth emits opening to switch
to the other tit.

That we sink into it, whatever we are,
whatever I am, nursing mother, postpartum
poet-on-pause, being suckled and holding,
sucking and being held, mother and daughter,

her mouth on my breast, my hand on her head,
our eyes on each other's.

That she drains me and I do not
even care, holding her there
in the time-stopped, milky darkness.

That the two of us are lovers.

That I love her.

That I love her more,
much more, than poetry.

That the cursor blinks blankly
at the end of an empty line.

Santa Caterina

Brian Doyle

Here's why I believe that indeed yes, a young woman in Italy once
Conversed at length with the One Whom No Name Can
  Encompass
In the year 1375 or so, by our calendar, although God knows which
Calendar the One goes by. He called her *dearest daughter*, you see?
That doesn't happen unless he really is a father. That's the real deal.
There's a fury of love for your kid, a tumult of feeling for which our
Words are flimsy. Like our words for the One. *Sometimes I pretend
Not to hear you*, he said to her, *but I do hear you*. Boy, I know these
Words. *Never lower your voice in crying out to me*, he says—*never
Stop knocking at the door*. I know this guy. He's a *dad*. His children
Drive him nuts and he would die for them without hesitation.
  This is
What I try to say to people when they say what's with the whole guy
On the cross thing, man, that's macabre, that's sick, you people look
At a guy dying of torture every day, you hang Him in your churches
And houses and offices, you carry a dying guy in your pocket, that's
Just weird, and I try to say he's a *dad*. He volunteered. You'd do the
Same for your kids. Sure He grumbled about it, in the garden. I have
Stomped down to the laundry room to snarl and throw shoes
  around.
But I go back upstairs because I love them more than I could explain.
They drive you nuts but yes you would die for them. I know *this* guy.

12

Conjugating

Judith Valente

I was the only public
that September at St. Aloysius

third desk from last
the alphabet outskirts of class

only Jane Zaccaro,
Barbara Zombrowski farther asea

My body a stranger
in alien clothes:

pleated skirt, white knee
socks, Peter Pan collar

buttoned to the neck.
In freshman art

Mrs. Cirone asked us
to observe a beechwood

describe what we saw
and some said summer

others said nature
I said the branches

were the serpent tresses
of Medusa—

—we had read
Bulfinch's Mythology

in Sister Helen Jean's
Latin class—

the bark the terrible
wide stem of her neck.

Mary Smith grimaced
Doris Crawford, then

Maureen Jennings
snickered, their laughter

washed over the waste baskets,
George Washington's portrait

the crucifix above
the blackboard in Room 202.

I wanted to run from that place
in my stiff new regulation loafers

from the girls who lived
in the stone houses on Bentley

and Fairmont Avenues
summered at Avon-by-the-Sea

knew by heart the Apostles' Creed
the Joyful, Sorrowful

and Glorious Mysteries
but I knew my mother

at that moment stood ankle
deep in red rubber boots

in a pool of gray water
hosing down cucumbers

at Wachsberg's Pickle Works
so she could earn $1.05 an hour

squirrel away a few dollars
each week to pay my $600 tuition

and at three o'clock
when Sam Wachsberg blew

his plastic whistle, remove
the boots, pack up her lunch sack

take home the Broadway bus
smelling of sweet relish

and pickled onions
while the school kids sniffed

her clothes, laughed
behind her back.

I learned to calculate the square
root of a hundred twenty seven

memorized the Holy Sonnets,
the symbols of the elements

mastered each declension
and conjugation:

amo, amas, amat

When, at Last,
I Meet My Mother Again

Jennifer Perrine

her face clotheslines me, that jolt closing
my throat, so I never get to say

I remember her as a dragon—
whoosh of leathery wings and hot wind

by my ear, a scritch of crimson claws
against the tile—or am I this beast,

the way I've swallowed her whole, scraping
each bit of memory from my teeth?

Yes, I am this serpent, the glinting
scales, the snap and flex of jaw, this worm

of furnace I call tongue that wriggles
free to cut her again and again,

not the way St. Margaret hacked out
from the devil's belly, but the way

the reverent divvy up a relic,
splintering bone from bone, chipping limbs

into holy slivers they'll cling to
when the rest of the body has gone.

Self-Portrait as St. Edith Stein

Susan L. Miller

From the train window, I watched my sisters' white palms
waving as long as I could see them. Pale roses for the Queen
of Heaven filled the cabin, headed with me to Cologne.

At home, my mother did not appear in the window to wave,
though we would not see each other again. The knowledge
of her disapproval lumped in my stomach like hard bread.

Weeks ago, when I had to face the grille and sing, I quailed.
I was more terrified to sing that hymn to Mary than when
I lectured to a crowd of a thousand students, but God

soothed me. Though shy, I did not strike a single sour note.
Weeks later, when I returned from my final visit home,
the Sisters received me kindly with white chrysanthemums

and buttoned me into my bridal gown, crowned with tulle.
We all marry our beloved Christ, and our habits frame every
expectant face. Now I have many sisters, Jewish and Christian,

and though we do not always understand each other,
God grant me the patience and love to speak well
so that I can translate between two mother tongues.

The Saints of April, 2005

Susan Settlemyre Williams

If April is an open door, the Pope
has just passed through, and it's about to slam
behind my mother-in-law. At her bedside
I'm browsing an old book called *Lives*

of the Saints. Mine. Mom's taste is for love
stories. She passes so gently through sleep
and waking these last days. Still carefully coiffed,
her white hair sets off a face turned suddenly

yellow-green. Willows are greening up, but slow,
and no one expected the old ones to hang on
so long. Easter's too early this year, Passover late,
month of fools and showers, bull chasing ram

down the zodiac. Bernadette of Lourdes appears
mid-April, St. George the week after, Virgin
pursued by dragon. Expectations are tossed around
like shadows the wind flings over a dazzle

of new grass. It's easy to be blinded,
blindsided. (Who is the saint of unwanted gifts?)
And now Mom's giving me her blond jacket.
I think you can wear it, she announces, a whisper,

but firm, instructs me I will love its warmth.
She's had it fifty years, but *timeless,*
a coat like that. Her husband, young and cocky,
negotiating at the fur farm. *Custom-made.*

He chose the minks himself. She doesn't explain,
but I want to know if he was shown a rack

of pelts or live animals romping in their runs.
I knew this was coming, planned not to look—I'd

donate it untouched to PETA, keep myself pure.
It means so much. I slide it from the zipper bag.
The outer fur more bristly than it looks,
silk lining and label faded. For Mary of Egypt,

converted whore and one of April's solitary saints,
a lion dug her grave in the sand—she'd lived
in the wilderness fifty years. Perfect tawny skins.
Were they after all allowed to romp? One scratch

and they would be unfit. April 8 is the feast
of St. Walter, *invoked for deliverance of prisoners.*
Walter the reluctant, appointed abbot over his own
protests, escaping over and over to live alone

in the wilderness, in prayer. Again and again
his order hauled him back. The Pope instructed him
to perform his duties *under threat of anathema.*
It would help me now to know if Walter was sainted

for his obedience or his running away. *I'm unfit,*
he pled. *Unfit*, I want to tell her, *for your gift.*
Instead, I slip my arms into the sleeves, clutch
the collar and, before her and the mirror, pose and turn.

Nicaraguan Morning Grounds

Rebecca Lauren

Or suppose a woman has ten silver coins and loses one. Does she not light a lamp, sweep the house and search carefully until she finds it? And when she finds it, . . . [she] says, "Rejoice with me; I have found my lost coin."
—*Luke 15:8–9*

When the sun broke open on the village's closed lids
it blazed bright as Nicaraguan housepaint,
stretching *rosada y naranjada* over the fat earth
like Marianela's housedress over her pregnant belly.

Early, she bent over the coffee grinder to pestle beans
for the dark morning brew by hand. Her oldest boys
rose when it was still night, brushed their teeth
with clean ash from *el fuego de ayer*. The little ones

still slept, three to a straw-stuffed mat, breathing in
the last cool breaths of *noche ante día*. That morning,
all I wanted to know were her *manos*, her marble plunk of beans,
the rustle of *granos de café* sifting to her metal catching pail.

From her yard of mango trees and *gallinas* pecking ground,
I wavered, unsure of how to ask for coffee after dawn
in a country not my own. It was harvest time
and Marianela knelt on the hard dirt floor to pray

against excess rain, against the middleman she knew
by swagger. I should have creaked open her screen door
and offered confession: Forgive me, *Madre*, for I have sinned.
But she absolved me before I could speak, blessing me

with a black-toothed grin of grace, washing me
blanca and awake with a cup of dark, bitter *café*.

I slipped round *pesos* between pages of her *Biblia*
when she turned to check on the *niños dormidos*,

as penance for Reagan, for Iran contra, for the *café*
I knew I'd buy for too little at the airport. Mornings later,
when the sun expanded over the same lines of longitude,
stretched to her sons' faces in the fields and mine in my bed

I knew she'd lift her worn *Biblia* from the rocking chair
and ease herself down to the woven seat, which held her weight
like a hammock. She'd pray to Saint Anthony for so many lost things,
then remember *niños dormidos* and pink-orange sun-walls

Goza conmigo, she'd whisper in gratitude
while coins in their multitude scattered across her dirt floor.

The Story I Like Best about Saint Teresa—

Susan Blackwell Ramsey

the spunky Spanish one, not the Little Flower—
isn't the angel and arrow vision Bernini
rendered so literally, orgasmic gasp
making him spiritual pornographer,
making us voyeurs caught peeking mid-cathedral.

And it's not the one of Teresa stuck in mud
axel-deep on her way to try to haul
some convent full of fashionable widows
toward reform, drenched, the pretty spitfire
shouting at the clouds "If this is the way
you treat your friends, no wonder you have so few!"

No, the detail I like is that, rapt in prayer,
she tended to levitate. She derided the pious,
scorned trances, always insisted the holiest nun
was the one you'd never notice, just doing her duty,
so floating embarrassed her. She'd grab the grille,
assigned other nuns to sit on her skirts, hold her down.

Nothing stopped it. Up she'd go. God as Lover
shocks Protestants, though it has a long tradition.
But this suggests God as Flirt, maybe even
God as Supreme Tease, pushing Teresa's buttons
for the fun of watching her sputter, knowing exactly
where they were located, having installed them himself.

Waiting for Ecstasy

Angela Alaimo O'Donnell

"Oh! no, you will see . . .
It will be like a shower of roses!"
—St. Thérèse of Lisieux

Day fades from gray to gray
while I stand here sorting colors:
hot whites, cold reds,
lukewarm blue and beige.

Prostrate before the cross,
heart pressed to the stone ground,
God speaks to her in roses
as the pail cools beside her,
the sodden sponge floating to the top.

I turn the dial and push.
Water fills the empty washer.
The force that moves my world, mute,
flows through power lines and circuits,
whose killing bolt can split a beating heart.

She lies still a long time,
knees and shoulders stiff,
crushed breasts numb,
her face a sun of love
in the blackened chapel.

Our clothes writhe and twist like the damned,
shells of our selves wrung and spun,
habits of our fanatic being.
I do little. I get nothing done.

Circling the cellar,
hands idle and empty,
I waste the hours
waiting for ecstasy.

In the Shower,
She Sees White Roses

Annette Spaulding-Convy

A wet thigh, neck, soapy red hair,

she finds her body here—
places she can't even name anymore,
her veil and scapular draped over the toilet.

She would die for a full-length mirror
to see if her butt is really as big as it feels,
if fasting cures more than just the soul.

Saint Catherine did it well,
years of communion wafers and water,
bedridden, but holy and lean.

And Catherine got something else—
four hours of ecstatic union with God,
who must have been pleased by what he saw,

a woman dying to be with him.
When hot water hits the curve of her back,
sometimes flowers rise from porcelain tiles

and she wonders if he is here—
a bouquet or at least a corsage
to pin on her small breast.

Portrait of Myself at Fourteen, as Saint Rose of Lima

Jennifer Perrine

Girl, I understood your temptations, your coveted face
rubbed down to red meat, the chili peppers scrubbing your cheeks

of each suitor's caress, shedding the glimmer of your skin,
your delicate hands, the ones you plunged wrist-deep into lime

then shoved in gloves full of nettles. How I envied your crown
of roses entwined with metal spikes, your hair-shirted world—

I had to make do with the tools of my time: the steak knife
I slid across my arms and ankles, anywhere their eyes

touched. When the first one came for me, I crawled into the cold
brick of my bed, waiting for a sign: I knew I'd been cleansed

when my blood dried up, when my hair cascaded from my head
in fistfuls of feathery wisps, when I could run my palms

over the flat of my chest and taste your words in my spit
like a bitter herb: *only pain keeps the Devil at bay.*

Poem

Kathleen Rooney

I am lying this morning
supine on your kitchen table,
pennies warming against the lids
of my eyes, because St. Paul says
we die every moment, so we can
disarm death by rehearsing it.

I am trying to act out my end,
a perfect tragedy, exhausting
the passions of terror and pity,
because events which themselves
we view with pain, we delight to contemplate
when reproduced with minute fidelity.

I am hoping you'll say something
about how you'll miss me. Eternally.
Instead, you sit down with a bowl of Cheerios
and tell me tragedy confines itself
to a single revolution of the sun. Then I'm back
to where I started from: adlibbing. Afraid.

Patron Saint of Worry

Kelli Russell Agodon

For an hour we complained
about Wiccans, about saints,

about the fact no one had invented
a babyproof lock for the bathtub faucet.

You said one morning you found
your two-year-old waist deep
in the tub; you were still

in bed, had slept late, a tired mother
who three years later, carries this guilt.

We hadn't even considered hot water,
the chance of third-degree burns.

For an hour, we said much
of our anxieties are from
being Catholic, from mothers

who grabbed for baseball bats
at the slightest sound.

You said your mother made you keep
your two fingers on the panic button

of your home's alarm while she explored
the basement, made sure no intruders
were around.

We still hear noises.

We still say grace
at the holidays.

We still pray though worry
we're hard to please.

You asked me how my daughter
knows her spirit animal is a heron
and how mine is a kingfisher.

I said I've sometimes traded saints
for totems, though

I still wear a St. Pio medallion
around my neck: *Pray, hope, and don't worry.*

Tell me if one day we will live
without carrying our history of grandmothers
next to the mace in our purse,

if we will sleep without thinking,
there's a door we forgot
to lock. You wear a locket of your son

and think up inventions
for hazards. I want us to invent a god

who hands out winning lottery tickets,
who wakes us each morning
from a dream about a solstice

party with good hummus and red wine,
and tells us there is a forest
of doors we need to unlock.

In the Voice of a Minor Saint

Sarah J. Sloat

I came at a wee hour
into my miniature existence.

I keep my hair close cropped
that my face might fit in lockets.

My heart is small, like a love
of buttons or black pepper.

On approach, I notice how
objects grow and contours blear.

That's what comes of nearness.
I have an ear for the specific,

as St. Apollonia minds the teeth,
and Magnus of Fussen, hailstones.

I dwarf gloom with my cachet sign:
one good hand conceals

my one good eye,
halving all disaster.

Sotto Voce

C. Dale Young

The humidity, somewhere around 95%,
simply would not allow the steam to lift
in generous curls from the street that day.

Instead, a dirty pool lay in the center
of the intersection, something dark
at the crossroads. Any minute,

some half-naked Augustine would take his place
center stage, dripping with spray-bottle sweat,
his right fist beating his chest:

Mea culpa, Mea culpa, Mea culpa.
Afternoons so slow in their departure
simply begged to be entertained, and so

my friend and I rolled around in bed, fully clothed,
mimicking one of a dozen sordid scenes:
always the imitations, the assignments

to be fulfilled—each verb precise, each
adverb filled with practiced lust—
our sin rehearsed until it was flawless.

Anonymity

Meredith Kunsa

On the street a generator clanks and growls.
A plastic sack slaps against the fire escape.

I disappear underground into the metro, push
through the turnstile. Doors wheeze open.

An old barber pole on Powell spins even when
it's not moving. The Bay Bridge holds up the sky.

This city of girders and glass is its own temple,
codified in graffiti. At noon people surge

into street canyons, queue up at cafes and metal
carts. Workmen eat from paper bags.

On a corner, the legless man sits on the sidewalk
watching his blanket of watches. Outside a boarded

church, Christ hallucinates in his hooded parka
preaching to pigeons fornicating on the steps.

Yellow tape across an alley, traffic halted, I see
my first dead man, his eyes pearled wide, neck

open. I am like Thomas the doubter, touching
the city's wound. Someone turns to follow.

I pretend to be unafraid. When our eyes meet,
we do not look away.

What Physics Teaches Us

Gerry LaFemina

In paintings of St. Peter, in figures of him placed in church
   alcoves,
he always looks the same; robed & standing on the large stones,
golden keys to the church in his hand,

but in the Bible where my baptism is recorded
& where my mother scratched out the record of my parents'
   wedding

there's a picture of St. Peter's crucifixion,
of the Roman soldiers lifting the cross upside down
because he refused to die the way his master had. I picture him
   though

the day after Christ's death, his guilt & remorse,
thinking of his wife, miles away, celebrating the Passover alone,

& how he hadn't thought of her for so long.

Really, I'm thinking of my father as I never knew him:
living alone in a studio & trying to sleep without my mother,
wanting a forgiveness he'd never ask for,

wanting, at least, his childhood dog that jumped in bed each night
& licked his salty face while he said *No! No!*

Does he think this his penance? Did he pray then, staring at the
   dark ceiling
& the patch of streetlight creeping through the drawn blind,

for sleep? For sin? The record spinning on the stereo
the way there's always a record spinning. Pop & hiss. The way
physics tells us the universe is spinning—radio waves & micro-
    waves &
remnant light. Numerous dimensions

so that Peter in his cell happens simultaneously with my father's
    longing
or my own
or happens again & again when we think about it
so when the priest thinks about Peter while fumbling keys to enter
    the church,

& turn on its lights & the church bells, his fingers on each key like
    a Rosary,

when the priest does this, Peter reestablishes his church
repeatedly, & Judas kisses the belly of his last harlot goodbye
& the kid in the classroom watching this could be me

thinking about Suzette Collins or my father or my mother laugh-
    ing at a priest's jokes,
which means I could be 13, or 33
& stopped in the second floor of Bush Antiques on Magazine
    Street, New Orleans
staring at a statue of St. Pierre

red splash of—is it paint?—on his wrists and ankles.

Twelve Days Before Christmas

Susanna Rich

Neighbor's halogen drives desperate tree shadows,
like too-many-fingered hands to me,

by my French doors, waiting, with her,
for her husband pursuing his high beams
too late and too long home.

St. Lucy plucked out her eyes
to be unlovely to all who cannot see.

Lucifer was banished not for darkness,
but that to darkness he might bring
a too unrelenting light.

Blessing

Angela Alaimo O'Donnell

In the doorway of the empty house
the woman waits, night silent outside,
learning how to say goodbye.

The floor shines wet in the moonlight,
mop in her left hand, bucket at her feet,
right hand resting on the brass knob.

Propped up in the wood telephone box
gleams the cross of San Damiano,
the one that gave good Francis the stigmata.

Alabaster Mary stands straight
in the arched niche beside it,
her infant son slung loose against her hip.

The woman's car idles in the dark
filled with her household belongings.
Her grown son sounds the horn, twice.

In Pope-like gesture, she signs
the room, echoes the words in the blue note
to the couple and their child who enter

this same doorway eight hours later.
They do not hear the blessing in the air.
They do not see the blood on the lintel.

Fathom

Erika Meitner

A large man holding his arms
fully outstretched is the nautical unit
of depth. Out of mine, I was buried
up to my ears.

Gertrude of Nivelles, the patron saint
of the recently dead, was renowned
for her hospitality—that's why
I let you in.

Wake me if you still want me, you said.
I wish my words could raise you
from your cardboard grave, arms reaching
toward the sky, towards me.

This August is so humid the door's wood swells
to fit the frame, making entrance difficult
and exits nearly impossible unless I kick it—
swift, hard, so it shudders.

My door a slab ripped
from its hinges. The parade of your body,
arms splayed out like blue sawhorses

police erect across intersections,
the proud T of their arms
holding back jubilant crowds.

Dominic Savio, patron saint
of juvenile delinquents, died at fifteen saying,
What beautiful things I see.

The blue stretcher; your heart
open to the sky, backs of your knuckles
scraping the cement walk.

Proximity

C. Dale Young

I have forgotten my skin, misplaced my body.
Tricks of mind, a teacher once said: the man
with the amputated right arm convinced he could

feel the sheets and air-conditioned air touching
the phantom skin. There must be a syndrome
for such a thing, a named constellation of symptoms

that correspond to the ghost hand and what it senses.
This morning, I felt your hand touch me on the shoulder
the way you would when you turned over in your sleep.

What syndrome describes this? Not the sense of touch
but of being touched. Waking, I felt my own body,
piece by piece, dissolving: my hands, finger by finger,

then the legs and the chest leaving the heart exposed
and beating, the traveling pulses of blood
expanding the great vessels. The rib cage vanished

and then the spine. If your right hand offends you,
wrote Mark, cut it off and throw it away,
for it is better for you to lose a part than to lose

the whole. But I have no word for this phantom
touch, and the fully real feeling of the hair
on your arm shifting over my own as your hand

moved from my shoulder and out across my chest.
Desire makes me weak, crooned the diva,
or was it Augustine faced with his own flesh?

Whisper me a few lies, god, beautiful and familiar lies.

A trap for St. Augustine

Maged Zaher

We learn about madness: about words walking as ghosts.
The choice of verb tense will control your shadows and the
extent of what you can promise your family. Weekend sex
will not turn into geography, tell them that, and tell them
that you are dead to the world, Augustine, and go on the
wagon.

But remember that the two paths are not as parallel as you
think. So spread the dense metaphor over multiple pages.
(We might finally convince someone of heaven.)

Passion

Eliot Khalil Wilson

I pounded nails through her creamy palms
and impossibly arched feet.
She never screamed, bled, or healed
—my breasted, blonde, pink Jesus—
—not a doll at all—but a gendered totem.

I had what you'd have to call a passion.

Before the microwave,
before the Whirlpool trash disposal,
I'd stuff her down the gaping mouth
of my father's mounted terror-eyed fish
so that only her white hair would show
in a narrative called *Barbie and the Rabid Bass.*

Or she would burn and melt in the furnace.
Her chemical skin blackening
in *Barbie: Virgin Bride of the Volcano.*

But I'd generally have her crucified.
My sister would find her, pull her down,
go weeping like Mary Magdalene
to my parents.

Always a new Barbie would appear in her cellophane casket
with her turquoise frying pan or neon pink vacuum.

Zealous, I continued to nail her everywhere I could—
—the tree by the bus stop, under the grape arbor,
the telephone pole, out by the mailboxes—
but I couldn't save her.

Always my sister would pull her down,
and make her play her truly suspect games:

Give her to Kubla Ken, Sheik of the Sandbox,
who would rescue her from white slavery,
give her a patio, fashion shop, dream house.

A disdainfully rich and powerful man,
Ken would force himself upon her
in what you'd have to call a marriage.

Ode to Saint Barbara
of the Barbara Shoppe

Rebecca Lauren

Oh bright, bombastic siren of follicles
with interchangeable crowns of auburn fire
light copper red and ginger honey blonde
you make a living by resurrecting our masses

of dead, snaky skin. Bless us, your patrons
with shears. Baptize us with holy hairspray
before we go into the world and preach
the gospel with a fixed bouffant of faith.

Wise Seer of Scissors, the first thing you learned
at beauty school was to cut by touch and not by sight.
With Cosmas and Damian, you joined
the throng of saints and blind barbers

those who never looked back
into the mirror, never asked *who is the fairest?*
Just swiveled and pumped parishioners
higher and higher, day after day.

Beatific Barbara, Blessed One of Natural Waves
when St. Martin de Porres visits you
after closing time and asks for a trim
you close your eyes and run a delicate razor

down the nape of his neck, loosen his locks
with a wide-tooth comb in the dimming Damascus light.
You are Sampson. You are Delilah. You are too good
of a Catholic to call yourself a priestess.

Too soon, he is gone and you stand alone
before your vanity's blinking mirror, snipping locks
from the crown of your own head,
then sweeping surrendered strands into a dustpan.

You discard your robe for street clothes.
You dip your fingers in holy water to loose the remnants
of dried mousse that hide beneath your fire red nails.
Then, in the afterglow of saints, you pray for our souls.

Saint Francis at Yoga

Susan Blackwell Ramsey

Back row, brown shirt, bald spot, smile
which gets wider when the teacher calls
the eating body *breath sheath*, says *inhale*.
Body, breath, energy—he's at home with threes.

During inversions he laughs right out loud—
a whole new world to praise! And he's illumined
by Sun Salutation, brother to Brother.
No stranger to prostrations, he could go on
all day, exalting, bowing, palms together.

He's always called his body Brother Donkey,
so Cat, Cow, Eagle, Downward Facing Dog
are no stretch except to hamstrings taut
from long nights kneeling. He loves Happy Baby.

When the teacher chants in Hindi he thinks this must
be how Latin sounds to peasants, and when it ends
Peace. Peace. Peace. it's hard for him
not to answer *Et cum spiritu tuo.*
He excels at Corpse Pose, Savasana,
the lips of his stigmata chanting Om.

St. Pachomius of the Unemployed

Alessandra Simmons

In the fashion that St. Pachomius
divided the labor of his monks so
I divide my day. Wake & Coffee
assault me with the light of a window.
Eat & Write, Walk & Shop
fellows with twisted hands, sweep
their limbs in bows before me.
We need mozzarella & bread
they remind me, we need a bag
& new underwear. I write it down.
At the library, St. Pachomius
does not wander. Marching up
& down the rows he levels
all the book spines. I'd tell
him, Relax, relax. But I've been split
between proofreading & sending
out copies of my resume
to draught-lands & incantations.
When I meet my quota
I lead St. Pachomius to the park
with a track where the laid-off
& third-shift workers play soccer
in the afternoon. Their goals are slain
trashcans, set ten strides apart.
St. Pachomius wonders aloud,
Where is the plow? If we walk,
should we not also work? There
are no plows in this city, I scoff.
Just tie up your robes & run.
The muscular St. Pachomius,
though still confused by the sixth lap

keeps pace with me in his
kindness & rolled-up dress.
The clouds, though bright
& far off, mist our cheeks,
our foreheads. St. Pachomius smiles.
The parsley is in the hand
of God today, he says, hold
flat your palms. After showering,
we board the train to downtown
where the high ceilings
of the Foundation welcome
anyone. Tonight a Nobel winner
reads her work in German & English.
The chairs are close together,
filled with students & dignitaries.
St. Pachomius though quite tall
sits beside me, legs folded, requiring
little room. As the author reads
an account of labor camp, her metaphors
ache in St. Pachomius. Though
the audience is dressed in pearls
& suits, the saint weeps without bowing
his face. After the reading he will not
join the crowd eager for wine & cheese.
I swallow a glass of white, pocket
a napkin & a finger sandwich. Back
on the train St. Pachomius runs a finger
over the seat edge in front of me, as if
to dust it. With his nail he scrapes
at the marker graffiti, the stains.
I tell St. Pachomius to stop—
that cleaning the train is not our job
but in his locked-jaw, he persists.
He pulls the corner of his sleeve to spit
shine the window then stands & moves

to the next, working the frame of the train.
Though no words pass, all the travelers
step out of his way. He begins to gather
trash with his hands. When train arrives
at our stop, I call out to him but he does not hear—
he kneels beside a far seat, reaching
for something I can not see.
I disembark onto the platform, empty
but for a mother & her sleeping stroller.
In whispers, as I walk, I list what I must do tomorrow:
again to the library, again to the track
I'll retrace the rows of books, push a few spines
out of line, set a few on their sides.

The Special Guest

James Tate

Down the chimney came old Saint Nick, which
was weird, because it was noon on a hot July day.
He was covered in soot. "Well, this is quite a
surprise," I said. "You should get that thing
cleaned," he said. "We weren't expecting you at
this time of year," I said. "You wouldn't happen
to have a beer, would you?" he said. "It's so hot
in this suit you wouldn't believe it." "Sure, I
can get you a beer," I said. When I returned, he
said, "Where the hell am I, anyway?" I told him,
and he looked confused. "Do you know what day it
is?" he said. I told him, and he looked bewildered.
He took a long slug of his beer. "I hate to admit
it, but I'm not really sure what year it is," he
said. I told him, and he thought about that for
a long time. "Can I have another beer?" he said.
When I returned, he said, "Why am I dressed like
this? It's hot out there." "You live in the North
Pole. You're only supposed to come down here
at Christmas." I said. "Oh," he said. "Mrs. Claus
died. I'm lonely up there. I want to live down
here, in a nice little house like this one." "Do
you have any money, some savings perhaps?" I said.
"I'm broke," he said. "I gave it all away, I
have nothing." "You could get a job," I said.
"I'm too old, and, besides, I don't know how to do
anything," he said. "We have a spare room, now
that the kids have gone," I said. "You could live
here and help out with odd jobs." He looked around.
"Could I have another beer?" he said. I got it
for him. "I just want to get out of these old

49

clothes, and shave this damned beard. It's too
hot," he said. He really did look miserable.
"Well, you can borrow my razor, and maybe we can
find you some summer clothes at Mr. Big's in the
mall," I said. "I'm just skin and bones," he said.
"There's no meat on me. I haven't eaten in months,
maybe years, I don't know," he said. "Well, then,
maybe some of my clothes might fit you," I said.
"I'd like that," he said. "I'd like to be able
to walk down the street without people making such
a fuss." After another beer, Nick shaved and tried
on one of my shirts and a pair of cotton slacks.
He was a gaunt, old man, who stayed in his room
most of the time. He seemed to not remember his
old life at the Pole, so Jill and I never mentioned
it. He liked to rake leaves in the fall, I don't
know why. Jill knitted him a sweater, and he cried
when she gave it to him. Then he kissed her, and
I said, "That's enough."

Saint Nicholas and My Party Guests Do Double-Takes

Maryanne Hannan

On the way to my 60th birthday party, I look
down, realize I'm wearing one brown shoe,
another blue, one low heel, the other high.

What will people say? always the first question.
And how will I answer? In 18th Century Russia,
women of means addressed their confessors:

Sometimes I strayed from virtue's path
(but immediately hastened to return).
Sometimes I allowed bitterness to blight my

heart (but not beyond the fall of night).
Peasant women forgot the niceties. Confessed:
I slept with my husband's brother.

I stole food from my mother's cabinet.
I watched my sister die.
When my mismatched shoes, awkward gait become

party chatter, I'll respond: Relax, let's just say I don't
know who I am, or where I'm going. (Sometimes
I spit on graves.) More often I split hairs.

Parable

Gerry LaFemina

That night among the flotsam
& jetsam of my life & among, too, the blown debris
of the city, among the wreckage &
driftwood, among so many broken selves

I stepped into St. Dymphna's,
not a parish but a tavern, & there
lit the taper of a woman's smoke because
I hoped—well, you know . . . It was like being sixteen

again, in church, when I believed
piety might make me more attractive,
trying to make it with an usher's daughter.
Such were my indulgences—

how many White Russians did I buy
in hopes kahlua & vodka might make me more
something, in hopes that juke box soul
might allow the guardian angel I'd flipped off

to smile upon me? Outside was all detritus
& distress. When I returned from the men's room
she'd gone. Someone rang bells of laughter,
while neon signs glowed like apocryphal stained glass

mosaics of the haloed & sinful both.
Oh how I longed to be one or the other
that night, so many years ago,
in our bar named for the patron saint of madness.

If I Returned to Rancor

Joseph Bathanti

The view would not decline.
This time the people would be friendly,
inviting my wife and me
to their churches, remarking
at my child's beauty.
Litter would disappear.

The mills would reopen
and the second-shift girls,
taking break on the Main Street curbs,
would be paid well
and go home to husbands
who never thought of beating them.

The tanker that leaked sulphuric acid
into the Catawba at Redtown Trestle
would never have been allowed through town.
No unwanted pregnancies:
no guns, drunks.
Blacks and Jews'd be revered;
starving animals adopted.
On the Feast of Saint Francis,
there would be a parade,
and the streets renamed for the martyrs.
Even the hard-shell Christers
would vote straight Democrat.

I would become best friends
with the cuckolded cafe owner
whose blue plates guaranteed sorrow.
He'd one day come to me
as I hunched over a poem

and a mug of his grey coffee
and confess that all his life

he'd loved poetry, but his wife
had left him for the fry-cook—
a thousand years ago, it seemed,
when the restrooms were clean
of graffiti and the juke-box
stocked with tender love songs.

We'd embrace and weep together.
Thenceforth he'd accept my checks
without accompanying ID.
His woman would return
and they'd redesign the menu—vegetarian.
It would catch on; then smiling.
Disputes would be settled through discourse,
and the town's name changed to Reconciliation.
We'd stay forever.

The St. Vitus Dance
of the Factory Floor

Jim Daniels

*When thrown into the den of a hungry lion, the beast merely
licked Vitus affectionately. . . . Some 16th century Germans
believed they could obtain a year's good health by dancing
before the statue of Saint Vitus on his feast day.*

Ed in Dept. 53 painted gold foot-
prints on the factory floor
around his machine—like dance steps:
a pattern to keep him clean
while welding brake-line clips
onto axle housings.

He wore button-down shirts,
slacks, and the steel-
toed dress shoes of management.
Midnights—the foreman cared not.
Spotless Ed, poster boy
for Good Attitude
though it earned him
no more money
and less good will.

Why did we paint those foot-
prints black one night
when he wasn't there?
We cupped our hands
around the dark candle
of cruelty in the dank swirl
the sharp steel clamor.

The next day, we punched in
early to watch his wax face
melt into the numb stare
of the rest of us.

The Feast of Stephen

for Mary Charlotte Griffin

Joseph Bathanti

A deer stand knifes out of a blackened elm
in a field once held in cotton.
It is the day after Christmas,
the Feast of Stephen,
first martyr, who died praying
for those who stoned him.

On Grassy Island Road,
men with dead quail in their pockets,
lean on pickups, smoke,
and wave grudgingly at passing sedans.

The Star of David spins through a bird sky
that presses the blond earth
with a vast blue sleep,
shadowing tithed tracts
purchased with 18th century sterling
along the Pee Dee and Buffalo Creek.

Corn cribs and cypress cabins
bone into millstone grit;
crumbling grey rock cob;
burlap and buckram;
broken iron, hand-forged
by Ansonville selectmen now buried
in Bethlehem Cemetery.

In All Souls Churchyard,
along its walls of Smith
and Nelme family sandstone,
the stained glass blazes.
Candles burn across the cropland.

The Fannie Situation

Jamison Lee

"This is no authority for the abuse of [fr]ees[ias]."—Gertrude Stein

"True," I concurred, "fun to pull a pornographic picture from a
pelvic pocket and make a dirty joke about it, but it can be delicate,
a major risk, if your audience is an old lady from Ohio. For," I
held, "Ohio's old ladies are vehement, the manner of Confeder-
ate begrudged, and, with bare hands, are known to have beaten
deer to death." Here, I cite Fannie Zimmerman, who, despite the
detail of a shovel, reifies my claim with her defense of periwinkles,
freesias, hibiscus.

Let us now praise Fannie Zimmerman—
steward of beflowered grounds—
who caught the fawn entering her
garden, with an obvious intent: foraging.

Praise Fannie Zimmerman—defender
of the lawn, chief of the land—who foresaw
the need of a hardy garden tool for ambush
of one impudent, pastel-petal-tonguer.

Praise Fannie Zimmerman, discriminating
fawn-slayer, that the madam didn't pummel Pudu
deer, which hail from Ecuador, enough lowgrown
for to hide under fern—Ohio shovel, a clear mismatch.

Praised be Fannie Zimmerman, shovel advocate;
And may the trowel be praised as well. Sufficient
for a Pudu are a trowel. Also, I suppose, praise the
watering cans, enabling domestication of maidenhair fern.

(Deer like mice: another place and time are
the "chevrotains,"—literal French: "little goat.")

Praise the mangled mess of blood and displaced
fur. Baby mice are not allowed to loiter in my aunt's
   driveway. For, like Fannie, she is old, and she
sometimes needs a favor; that is to say, I, too, know
how wood vibrates as on soft bones fall shovels.
And, while it's true that a couple errant swings
made metallic onomatopoeia (asphalt-black
dissonant xylophone), Fannie Zimmerman,
shepherd of deer skull, she absorbed a rattle
sturdier than mine, which were blind and cheep
cheep. Her initial inquisition required guile.

Praise thus Fannie Zimmerman, conservationist,
creeping toward the bedlamic bushwhack: short
bleating efforts to summon a mother doe, ruptured
by the tin baritone clang made on the tawny,
developing head. (Praise Fannie at full blitz.)
Then deeper, wetter claps. Wheezing through
a yogurt throat. Leg spasms. Eyelids grasping.

Praise Baron Zimmerman, sentinel of flower patch,
perennial custodian, curator of deer corpse. Green
thumb. Skull-crushing, cleaner than digging neck-hole;
yet looming: heavy work deer-scrapping.
Praise the winded contemplation, internal dialogue:
removal of fawn carcass, how to . . .

Praise Sister Zimmerman, janitor of fawn blood,
with dirty hands, like the Amish, who are like Fred Astaire
with a shovel, though what really comes to mind
is the Yankee who retaliated, shot the fleeing Amish boy
whose older brother had given a truckward volley
of tomato. Praise the rebuttal of an airborne tomato.

And praise airborne tomatoes. The Spanish crack
of gun conjuring catapults kicking off *La Tomatina*.
Every year on the final Wednesday of August in Bunol,
Valencia, Spain, they throw overripe tomatoes by the ton.
La Tomatina is a paratelic festival, the bandying of fruit
its essential composition. Praise the fruited Spaniard,
her paratelic state, a state of playfulness. Praise
the Greek prefix, "para," meaning "separate from"
or "beyond." And the root, "telic," for "expressing end
or purpose." Praise paratelic buckshot heralding *Tomatina*,
held in honor of the town's patron saints: Hubertus and Giles.

Let us praise Hubertus, but ask not Fannie Zimmerman's
veneration of Giles, patron saint of beggars, lepers,
cripples. Greek emigre vegetarian hermit, circa late
seventh century A.D., Giles ducked in some Gallic
forest and was apparently sustained for years
by his lone companion, a small red doe, on the teat
of which he suckled. Expect instead for Fannie,
like I said, to honor Hubertus, patron saint of hunters.

And yet, here is Hubertus, a candid picture:
Noble from the North of France, harrying a buck
through the wood on Good Friday, circa 683;
intervened upon with divine instruction from a spectral
crucifix hovering between the stag's antlers. This man
studied a cloud of crucifix above a buck's head,
dropped his bow and let his quarry go, choosing
to become a priest instead. That Good Friday's pivotal hunt
effected Hubertus to castigate spelunking, rebuke
lovemaking, chide blue-eyed soul for
subsequent embrace of a disembodied riddle.

Confounding is the irony that this Hubertus,
who, beheld an apparitional, fluorescing antler-cross;
who remembered prohibition of Good Friday hunting;

who dithered home, quit archery to join a clergy;
is, nevertheless, the patron saint of hunters.
Despite vegan impulse, near-bestial fantasies,
the church identified the Hubert just described
as the patron saint of hunters, (and of archers!)
smelters, trappers, two cities in Belgium,
metal workers, mathematicians, opticians, and dogs.

So, Praise Fannie, canonical revisionist,
and . . . Hunters! who are we praying to? Really!
The teat guy? The vegan priest? Fannie was 75!
Got the job done with a shovel. I can't speak
for the Belgians, but this is a no-brainer, I think.

Pray, yes, to Fannie Zimmerman, I suggest,
or maybe my uncle, who got one with a crossbow,
had it butchered properly, and made a pretty good
salsa cheese dip. A little bit oily, and the meat
rather chewy. Still, at least my uncle is bestially
chaste, lips unacquainted at the nipple of a doe.

Anyway, in addition, praising, then, heretofore,
the shovels, trowels, watering cans, cheesy
salsas, patron saints, and whatever else, remember,
please: Praise the fruited Yankee.
Also, praise the shotgun: shovel of the fruited
Yankee. And the dead fawn: Amish boy of Fannie.

Double Saints Day

Helen Ruggieri

I'm wearing a chartreuse hoodie
and a Kelly green tee.
My socks are lime green.
Nobody cares today.
It's part of March Madness.
The St. Bonaventure brown Indians
are playing in the first round of the NCAA
for the first time in twelve years.
All the friars are praying for a win,
to up enrollment, to resurrect
a basketball program down on its luck,
to inspire alums and donors,
but they lose and St. Patrick
dead in Ireland a thousand years ago
is peat under the green green grass
of the auld sod and St. Bonaventure
is lecturing the seraphims.

II.

Faith and Worship

Faith

Maria Terrone

In the church vestibule I pass
the monitor that registers the bodies
of the faithful as gray
flickers, a second of ash
on a screen, and heave against the doors.
At 3 p.m. no one else is here but saints,
corporeal in their sandals and robes,
carrying staffs, books, painted bouquets,
their kind faces cracking
as if they too know
how it feels to come apart.

Wedged into the fingers of St. Jude
is a hand-printed prayer, a paper bud
curled so tight, I feel its plea
for a miracle tug the back of my throat:
cure the cancer, kick the habit—the ineffable
longing of a stranger's words alive
on my own tongue.

Days later, the hand holds instead
a shriveling rose stem.
Petals lie scattered about
like small, white-robed monks,
backs arched to heaven,
faces pressing stone.

The Angel with the Broken Wing

Dana Gioia

I am the Angel with the Broken Wing,
The one large statue in this quiet room.
The staff finds me too fierce, and so they shut
Faith's ardor in this air-conditioned tomb.

The docents praise my elegant design
Above the chatter of the gallery.
Perhaps I am a masterpiece of sorts—
The perfect emblem of futility.

Mendoza carved me for a country church.
(His name's forgotten now except by me.)
I stood beside a gilded altar where
The hopeless offered God their misery.

I heard their women whispering at my feet—
Prayers for the lost, the dying, and the dead.
Their candles stretched my shadow up the wall,
And I became the hunger that they fed.

I broke my left wing in the Revolution
(Even a saint can savor irony)
When troops were sent to vandalize the chapel.
They hit me once—almost apologetically.

For even the godless feel something in a church,
A twinge of hope, fear? Who knows what it is?
A trembling unaccounted by their laws,
An ancient memory they can't dismiss.

There are so many things I must tell God!
The howling of the damned can't reach so high.
But I stand like a dead thing nailed to a perch,
A crippled saint against a painted sky.

Desert Ascent
John of Climachus

Trina Gaynon

I.   At eighty he still scales the ladder to God; so long spent
     on the thirty rungs that he begins to doubt visions of angels—
     all halos and no legs, until demons take over
     his dreams—all ebony silhouettes—equipped
     with lassos and bows. He longs for solitude.

II. No wooden ladder mine, but metal, too short
     for heaven and leaning against the house in the rain.
     Once again I delay clearing the gutters until
     water drips down the bedroom wall.
     Alone, I scrape leaves from roof, gutter, downspout,
     shove them over the side, wondering if I can manage
     to hold the ladder steady as I step over the parapet
     to back down. All I want is down.

III. In the icon, those eager to be near
     Christ jostle John up his ladder. Do you recognize
     your face among the monks tumbling from the rungs?
     How high had you gone before a devil fluttered
     his wings and lured you off? Did he need
     his lasso or his bow and arrow? Or were you pushed?
     There are no temptations visible in the burnished gold leaf,
     just your reflection, created by protective glass—
     the monks and their companions held in the climb
     towards heaven,

               where it feels as though I intrude
     (my eyelashes as long as the monks are tall)
     though I've plenty of company: The patriarchs in the corner,

the pilgrims behind John, angels and demons, museum guests,
the priest who traveled from Sinai with the art.

Assured of one companion, dwelling in awe, and a panoramic
view of the rigorous Sinai, I might find it possible to grasp
a rung at shoulder height, put my foot on that first step.

Offering to Saint Roch

Melinda Palacio

Water rises. Rises over rooftops,
cars, schools, neighborhoods.
A town rebuilds. You're still a wreck.

Saint Roch cures all. In gratitude, leave
your plastered body part. But you want to offer
your whole body, not just a finger or a toe.

You pray to Saint Roch, ask for his help.
Receive a divine answer. Floating is
better than drinking in the morning.

When your FEMA money arrives, you ignore
your weathered house. You build a swimming pool
instead, as if floating will save you from another hurricane.

After Saying *The Chaplet of the Divine Mercy*

Karen Kovacik

Saint Faustina, Cinderella among nuns,
I climbed your words slowly
in my fragile armor, like a beetle
tired of dodging shoes.
Rung by rung I sang of mercy
"for myself and for the whole world,"
in tears then clear-eyed,
grateful to say your litany with others,
like after the Eucharist,
solitary in a crowded pew,
when words leave me
and I feel my hollowness
hum like the larch floors
you scrubbed on your knees.

Spokes

Kristina Roth

"I drive like I ride!" you exclaim with a laugh as you accidentally run a stop sign in the creaky blue van on our way to visit your elderly aunt in the nursing home. We'd cut rain-soaked iris for her from her own garden: the scent of anise, water droplets illuminating the curves of their pale lavender petals.

"Did you know it's just the spokes that hold us up? Just these little, thin spokes?" you asked when we were sixteen, bicycle tires whirring beneath us on a dark summer night, stars bright above in a June sky. Speeding down a hill was the best thing I knew, exhilaration rising in my chest as the wind blew around my face.

Now you speak of Saint Faustina and other saints I do not know. It's been twenty years and you still bike everywhere. Uphill and down, to work and to church, downtown and back, always in a skirt, a scarf in your pocket to wear at daily mass. My family members see you all over town.

"I finally bought another bike!" I will tell you when I visit this summer. "Dark red like the one I rode in high school." I fly through my suburban neighborhood, giggling at the fun I am having, at how far and fast I can go on these turning silver spokes. I am sure drivers are laughing at me, a fat lady on a bike, my flabby butt hanging over the seat, but I don't care. I think you would approve.

In a letter, you enclose a small card of the Divine Mercy image. I see the rays of light emanating from Christ's heart as they did in Saint Faustina's vision and I see bicycle spokes, spokes of mercy holding us up, keeping us from falling, supporting us as we spin through these dark streets, glimmers of light above.

Spiritual Exercises in a Cellar Bookstore

Brett Foster

Hide me within Thy wounds, Memory,
ennoble these afternoon passions—
a busy day, register down, down on my luck,

and in the corner of the store
at the back of the Spanish section
lies my dust-covered method perfectly

at home in perused silence. The thin leaves
composing the folio barely conserve
the fading *Imprimatur* of Paul III.

Last Sunday just before closing
I considered his cave meditations
to rid myself of "disordered tendencies."

I sought the divine Will, and at least found
some thrill of discipline; the physical
act channeled the spiritual like a funnel,

steered everything toward a single gesture:
each time one falls into that particular
sin or defect, let him put his hand

on his breast, grieving for having fallen.
I locked the store early and knelt
below its shoebox of a window, the sky

reminding me of our peculiar kingdom,
heirs of time and eternity, a dual dominion
shared not even with angels, a "singular privilege."

After the prelude, *evacutatio sensuum*,
the mind spilling through the body to clear
itself, vacuous, then the terminal flare

of Conscience, *applicatio sensuum*, the fiery
iron of the senses branding the composition.
Each heartbeat spans eons. The halted moment

elevates my small Understanding: the smell
of sweat and blood in the midnight garden,
the vinegared sponge of Golgotha—

and I can see you too, Ignazio, fallen
soldier, leg twice broken. Last sacraments
administered at Loyola castle,

you convalesce by reading legends
on the Bay of Biscay. On the altar you hang
your sword before the Virgin and pronounce

the vow, a celibate among the emerald
fields of Monserrat, clothed in a hemless
pilgrim's robe, voice robbed by your colloquy,

then turned to sterling. Your Society
proclaims you "trainer of men." The drama
of one body's cosmography—immediate world

willed from a little book—: heart, brain, vapors;
I burst before the mass of history . . .
gold silence of the shelves, dialogue of flowers

sprouting from marrow, and the mind
like white manna resplendent in the window,
the sweet stars of Manresa moving swiftly.

Blue Willow Plate

Victoria Edwards Tester

Yesterday I stole my blue willow plate back
from the old church in Mogollon
because I didn't want the Virgin
to make that cavalry officer turned car salesman
love me after all.
It would be bad luck to leave it there.
After all, I'd met you, the living half-deaf twenty-eight greats
grandson of Saint Francis.
Who they say was a real musician and carouser
until the tragic day the Holy decided to haunt him
in a voice like wild mint blowing on the sides
of a clean creek. Four hundred years later they boxed
that voice and sailed it here, to New Mexico,
to harass the bodies and souls of the plants and animals,
men and women. If anyone understands the pickle
of lust, it's Saint Francis.
So I didn't lower my eyes when I carried
my blue willow plate out of the church
they named for him. The empty clothes hanger
that wired the door shut was the horse
shape of your naked shoulders
and hips, riding me tonight, if you were willing.
Then the rickety wooden porch where I crossed
my fingers the Holy would keep His mouth shut.
For that silence, I thank the open yucca pods
I left on the altar. All those tiny black yucca seeds,
like the thousand pieces of the night sky broken
only by its lucky stars.

Song for Saint Nicholas Day

Terry Kirts

Another dim morning, I stare into my shoes.
The bishop has not visited me with his dowry
of peppermint, his sachet of bittersweet gold.
Instead, I'm forced to fetch my own hod of coal,
to pray the heat back to my apportioned space
while the rooftops rattle with nothing but wind.
Oh, to be like my grandmother as a girl:
sufficient with her orange, her licorice whip.
To dream while the paving stones cooled at my feet,
sleeping through each arthritic creak of the shanty's
frozen boards.
                    How un-Byzantine *my* wishes:
a bit of sun to read the paper by, a kitchen
someone else has cleaned. The gray day hangs
in windows like a confessional's opaque screen.
One candle to stave off longing and one to bring it back.
Could I have slapped the heretic howling before me,
burned idolaters' churches, saved the innocent three?

Deliberate as a cleric, I bake, remembering
the spinster aunt who wept endlessly
into her bowl of dough. She, too, was tortured
by her virtue, yet they knew her macaroons
all over town, dunked them like grace into
their grateful cups of tea. I push a dull thumb
into each compliant dollop, whisper a prayer
above the oven's hot gush. Later, like a child
                    of Brussels or Minsk,
I take my supper by light of the evening star,
sparing myself before another night's riches. In sleep,
for once, my tossing does not trouble me. I see

how I'll survive the years: his hand on the tiller,
the twin spires of his miter thwarting the storm.

Say My Name

Franz Wright

I'd be entombed
inside a period

in the closed book
in the huge dark

of St. Paul's
where we used to meet,

       wafted

downaisle toward
banked sunlight-colored candles.

I'd be in your mouth,
in that huger dark:

body that stands for the soul.

Word that means you are loved.

In Avignon

Ned Balbo

Petrarch sees "Laura" for the first time, April 6, 1327

In Avignon, the monstrance of St. Clare
In place above the altar, eucharist
Set high for all to see, worshippers blessed
Beneath transfigured flesh, I touched your hair,
Or would have, if I'd dared to come so near,
Ring scarcely visible. The moment passed,
But as the crowd swarmed through the doors, the best
Of what was left to me—more penance, prayer,
And poetry—rose up before my eyes,
One flash of light: one moment. When I see
You always at a distance, all the lies
I'll tell myself from now on, secretly,
Will fuse to one: transfigured flesh, a maze
Of passages, all dark, encircling me.

Agápe

Timothy Murphy

The night you died, I dreamed you came to camp
to hear confession from an Eagle scout
tortured by forty years of sin and doubt.
You whispered Vespers by a hissing lamp.

Handlers, allowing you to hike with me,
followed us to the Bad Axe waterfront
down a firebreak this camper used to hunt.
Through all I said you suffered silently.

I blamed the authors of my unbelief:
St. Paul, who would have deemed my love obscene,
the Jesuit who raped me as a teen,
the altar boy when I was six, the grief

of a child chucked from Eden, left for dead
by Peter's Church and all the choirs above.
In a thick Polish accent choked with love,
Te Dominus amat was all you said.

Absolution

Mary Jane Nealon

"I dream of an ideal confessor to tell everything to, spill it all:
I dream of a blasé saint."
—E. M. Cioran

I don't discuss impure thoughts and acts.
I want forgiveness for small abandonments:
my brother left alone after surgery to tie his own shoes.
My saint, apathetic, sits on a rock near me,
his gown falls between worn knees. He yawns,
he's seen worse: men drawn and quartered, women
burned at the stake. And then I leave him, even.

Infidelity, a gift I learn well.
I cheat on myself with myself,
confess my mixed emotions for the human body,
for the way I stand by and watch things happen.
For invasions, large and small: thin needles, chest tubes.
I watch primitive rituals and call them science.
I search the faces of the dead for answers—
Where have they gone to? Why are they cold?

My saint, meanwhile, signals me.
It's easy at the bedside of the suffering.
I'm good at what I do. But my sin is this:
I use the dying to understand where my brother has gone.
Each time I touch them I am studying their bodies
for clues. And the little prayers I say are always for myself.

Saint Joe Considers the Furnace

J. D. Schraffenberger

The furnace flares up, abrupt, a smell in the room
    like burnt dust, or smoked meat, an old sweater worn
    for a hayride bonfire and hung far back in the closet.
In warmth, troubling things turn sweet, the mind seizes
    on a fugue—worries get cute, mingle, flirt with the tune.
    Hello, Bach. Fine thanks. I've heard so much about you.
    What disappears will return and pain me later.
It's a simple habit, turning up the heat to 75.
    But in warmth, sweet sad things hatch in my breast.
    This says as much about me as any confession ever will,
    a house heated beyond comfort, *St. Matthew Passion*,
vague memories of the outdoors. When she is asleep
    and I turn up the heat, I think about the moist still
    dreams of warm places breeding behind her eyes.

Pentecost Sunday: Mátyás Church, Budapest

Susanna Rich

Coming late (almost not) into this medieval dusk,
I sit in the way-back of the church,
on stone steps leading down from the old

barricaded entrance—cold, here, where tourists
with single camera eyes, Christophers
with noisy toddlers, and the unaffiliated flock.

Haydn's *Kyrie* has pinioned the priest
to a sanctuary chair—he in his sure red chasuble,
I in my red voile dress—facing each other

from far ends of the nave.
The "Nelson Mass for Times of Distress"
is all trumpets, tympani, organ, and voices,

voices. How can I deserve their piercing fullness?
I'm tempted to flip open my Motorola to call
my sleeping husband—*come hear*—

as if his being lofted into this soprano's reach
would make me worthy to hear it, myself.
This 50th day after Easter that closes corner ABCs,

frees fathers to pocket playgrounds,
slows trams and the underground, I had only
silence from my laptop and sleeping husband.

My father died a year ago today in America—
while his friends prayed at Hungarian Mass.
Kyrie, Kyrie . . . so I have come this morning.

A baby burbles with the strains of music,
an ancient whacks his walker along the floor.
How can I find my father's Jesus in me?

The Blessed Mother rises above the altar
in a frankly vaginal frame. This vault, this
overturned ship is hers, but they call it

Mátyás's Church for the warrior, wealthy donor,
twice-married here, namesake of Matthew
who replaced Judas. My twice-married father

disavowed me as not Hungarian woman
enough—I who betrays him now by playing
at belief in the church he loved . . .

Big Sur Saints

New Camadoli Monastery
Feast of St. Benedict

Angela Alaimo O'Donnell

Christ called so loud, we left the lonely road
that rimmed the earth along the singing sea,
a gentle summons from a gentle Friend,
sweet promise of God's hospitality.
The monks were gathered on the mountain top,
the table set, their vespers just begun,
two spaces open on the altar steps.
The echo of the single church bell rung.

Here each man chanted his best hopes aloud
like sane men singing to a world gone mad,
and our two voices joined the joyful choir
in that strange place lit by ordinary fire.
We blessed and we broke. We spoke the ancient code.
We left the holy mountain. Bread and blood for the road.

Pilgrims

Erin Elizabeth Smith

I.

I wanted to come home,
it just took too long to find the right plane.
Two years of eating grapes meant for wine,
wondering where the skin goes
when the flesh is juiced and fermented.

Maybe I would have thought of us
less if France had been more than cheese
and yardstick bread, more than yellow countryside
like Illinois when the corn is tall.

II.

I forgot how days pass in New York—
stubborn mist shaking its mane on the highway,
snow that siestas in the sky for days.
His green towel, folded and hung
on the bathroom door, smelling so much like him.

III.

First it was Vezélay. Clutching the skirt
of Mary Magdalene, who told me of her years
of desert shelter—the crows, the sand,
the sucking cactus. There were no angels
that delivered her to Christ's oyster bar.
Just a jackrabbit she tore open with her hands,
blood she drank religiously.

Then Santiago de Compostela, where the hermit
found James under a transept of star,

his marrow drained, hair cleaned from skull. He waits
in stone sombrero, a staff cocked
in his left hand, a closed text in his right.
They think it's the Bible, he winks,
and that these are my bones.

Finally, Ravenna, blackcaps warbling
on the telephone poles. Just south
of the pinewoods strangled by heather,
dog-rose, I ordered wedding soup.
I was finished with leaving,
with Europe
with the thousand stone churches
that starved their towns.

IV.

Somehow this would make more sense
if there were myrrh or bdellium involved.
Because then he would laugh, open
his palms that clench and unclench at his thigh,
smile at the plastic snow globe
I bought in the Turin airport.

I look at him, but he is watching the planes
lift like storks from the sandbar willows.
Didn't you hear, he says when I ask
how the city has been. Christ came back
as a bamboo shark last week.
And the Devils brought home the Cup.

Saint Rita

Lorraine Healy

Santa Rita, lo que te da, te quita.
(Saint Rita, what she giveth, she taketh away.)
—*popular Spanish saying*

i

In Cascia, perched yellow
on an eastern Umbrian hill,

inside a crystal coffin, like a fairy tale
princess, dead asleep, is Rita,

patron saint of impossibles;
one dead foot impossibly flipped
back, the other laid on a cushion.

She is turning brown with time,
fully dead and incorruptible,

the kneeling faithful around
the wrought-iron grates, the crystal cases

containing babies' bibs and pacifiers,
those conceived in surprise and prayer,

or hammered tin in the shape of limbs,
of hearts, the tin *milagros* of the healed,

incense and spent wax hanging
in the blue air of her church.

ii

Seventy miles west, a waxen Clara of Assisi
sleeps in another crystal coffin,
plump and unreal.

In a different crypt, my mother
thinks she sees Francis' remains
in what looks to me like

a disheveled bird's nest,
which she insists is his skull.

Umbria is dotted with saints
and cypress and these impossible
golden towns perched on hills.

We go from Benedict to Scholastica
to Valentine, into crypts that smell
of mold and wet rock,

where the polychrome of the Madonna's feet
has been kissed away by years
of love and madly devoted hands touching.

We walk up the hot stone *vias*—indolent sun,
muted birds, the borrowed death of *siesta*—my mother carries
the invisible cross of her depression

to yet another church.

iii

On a baked July keeling towards
August, I saw so many of the pious,
their eyes celestial, blessed and woeful,
among them my mother, palm
against palm the way she learned in childhood;
and all were on their knees,

silently asking a browned corpse encased in glass
for some impossibility.

This, believe me, is how it goes:
the tiny corpse, its raisin face impassive,
has the ear of God, and God's favor.
She only *looks* immobile, peaceful.
Saints are those who spend their eternities
at work for others, relaying prayer
to God's symmetrical feet.
God is so busy. The saints insist:
"Hear me, hear me . . . This one's deserving."
In this place of air there are no
impossibilities. Rita tugs the Lord's sleeve.

iv

Rita the housewife who pined to be a nun,
three violent men who died young
freeing her for the convent, where she finally
dove into her love for Christ, who sent her

a ring of bleeding around her head,
his phantom thorns to Rita,
circular rubies of ache,
the Christ's terrible loving.

Five hundred and fifty years of this,
becoming a prune, a pit-less date
in the perfect house of her crystal
in the royal blue of her hideous church

on the stone of this Umbrian hill
amid the lame and the wheelchaired,
amid the steady pilgrimage of the broken,
all of us watching Rita's long sleep,

a tiara of bloody flowers around her head,
Rita at peace with her flipped foot
on a velvet cushion, what to ask
of her silence, what impossible prayer

dies in my chest while my mother kneels on the steps,
my mother mentally unfolding the long list
of her intentions, all of which
she lays at Rita's dead unsymmetrical feet

with the docile certainty of her faith.
And around us the old women in house dresses
clic-click rosary beads, candles' thread of thin black smoke,
will it dull the demented blue of the walls, I wonder;

will it sneak into the crystal case
and brown Rita's papyrus skin, how
would that be for impossible and what's a saint
to do with so much asking?

v

Outside, flapping in the scorching July breeze,
a parking ticket trapped by a windshield wiper
on our rental, punishment for stumbling

into the wrong parking lot after the green
switchbacks up this hill. My mother says,
see? Rita's already taking away.

Pilgrimage to St. Colman's Well

Meredith Kunsa

Seeking refuge from the world's ruckus,
I've traveled five thousand miles in footsteps
of the faithful to these Irish uplands

where rock chokes the landscape forming
stair-stepped gullies of stone. Two sheep dogs
join me at a farmer's gate then run ahead

through pastures and cobbled stiles, circling
back in their shepherding. As the ground rises,
a lone tree appears shading a pile of rocks

rimming the mouth of the well. Grass struggles
through cracks, bends to the flow of wind.
Within the well, clogged with ferns and nettles,

someone has placed a small plastic madonna.
In the sixth century, St. Colman found a hermitage
here. He brought with him a cock, a mouse, a fly.

The cock woke him for matins, the mouse
scratched his ear if he slept too long and the fly
marched along lines of his Psalter keeping his

attention on the text. From this font he was baptized
by two clerics—one blind, one lame. These two
sheep dogs, tongues lolling, must now serve

as my witnesses. I cup a palm from the spring
and press it to my lips. Sounds of lowing cattle,
a communion of wavering lament, spreads from

the valley like a healing elixir. Turning for home,
I leave behind as a pilgrim's offering, my name
written on the water.

Praying to St. Stephen's Hand

Susanna Rich

Can you feel his sure, tireless hand
amongst the leaves?

—from Sándor Csoóri's "Meghallod-e még?"

I grasp my grief and non-belonging
like a nosegay of paper poppies to
enter this Budapest basilica, pass the velvet-
covered cordon chain, show my ticket to
The Sanctuary of St. Stephen's Hand.

They call it *Szent Jobb—Holy Right, Holy*
Better—the left, beyond mouldering, with
Stephen's other parts, scattered, like memories,
almost a thousand years throughout Hungary—
ancient custom: dissect and bury the king over his

larger body—the land. Into the slot I slip a 100
forint coin—stainless steel ringing a brass core—
for my ration of illumination: an ossified fist lying
in a glass casket among gold acacia leaves—single
Christmas bulb dull. I'm too distracted by the guardian

in Roman collar (and my anticipation of the end of light)
to feel an awe to flatter myself, if momentarily, that I am home
with the Father—that he waits for me, that he might hold
the boy my father was, drifting on hillsides
espaliered with grapevines; and the girl who would

marry him, picking peaches into her apron. I am hungry,
here. On my knees. Cold. Always the import—west
of the Prime Meridian or east. Tongue dancing to

strains of someone else's music. I am the thief in diaspora—
camera around her neck, world web on her back.

Needing *what*? The claw of my father's hand lay
on the hospital sheet—gone was the ebony he hammered
of his thumbnails; gone, the fingers tying my laces.
What I have left: his reaching through my fingers, as if
through gloves, pressing them together, as if in prayer.

Seeing the Sights

Loretto Palace, Prague

Alice Friman

In the Chapel of Our Lady of Sorrows
a bearded woman hangs from a cross.
Her name—Vilgefortis, Saint Starosta,
who after taking a vow of virginity
was forced to marry the king. Whereupon
God, the All-Merciful, gave her facial hair
to make her less desirable.
You see where it got her.
                                    There she is
nailed to her five-o'clock shadow.
No weeping mother. No deposition.
No miracle in the tomb. She dangles
in her side-show getup, beyond tweezers
or depilatories, electrolysis or laser,
forty bucks a shot. Grind golden scissors,
strop a magic blade. It will do no good.
This is God's hair, tough as wire,
inspired as twisted nails.
                                    Do not think
the villain was the groom. Sicilian,
he knew his angel hair, and recognizing
in that tangle the design of heaven,
shopped for a colorist and curling iron.
Wooed her with ribbons, rinses, and the promise
of corn rows and beads.
                                    It was her Daddy
nailed her up, for what sort of daughter
needs hormone replacement therapy at fifteen?
And who could bear the disappointment

of one's own pussycat turned dead ringer
for Methuselah? So he crucified her,
hammered her back to God, while her betrothed,
that noble Sicilian from Palermo, wept
and itched in his hair shirt for the miracle,
the burning bush that was almost his.

Apocalypse Island

Nicholas Samaras

I remember the yawning port at two a.m.,
the gold necklace of street lamps draping the dark.

I remember the night-shawled grandmothers leading us
back to rooms to let, sleep crashing onto us

like the black-laced surf outside the open window.
I remember the happy weariness of traveling homeward,

the shades of ancestors nodding. I recollect
the morning that broke gold light all over the room,

the Patmian cove new again. I remember scrambled
food for nourishment and the whitestoned monastery

hovering over Skala's bolt-blue sky. I remember Nikita and me
climbing the pine-green mountain. I recall our youth.

Halfway up the mountain path, we came to a sign
nailed to an olive tree, a white sign in the rough

shape of an arrow, inscribing "This way to the Apocalypse."
And my stunned translation, hysterical with laughter.

I remember the steep hillside on which Nikita and I
sat for breathing amid the saffron of wild flowers.

I had the barest of hands, wide with nothing, and so
braided wild blossoms, stained my fingers and heart

yellow with them. I walked the corolla chain to the Cave.
I remember the coolness of the air as we entered

the chapel of his Cave—Saint John of the Revelation.
All of my future was ahead of me. I framed

the twine of flowers around the ancient gold icon
and walked back into light, both empty and full.

Astoria

Dean Kostos

I shuttle toward singed-meat air,
toward honeyed cafés & late cigarettes.
In a church, women plant candles

in sand—ghostly flowers in a garden.
Wielders of light, let me take refuge
among the petals. Let forsythia

speak a waterfall of fire.
The Virgin's icon weeps
myrrh. I trail her fragrant tears.

Saint Spyridon materializes
from a mosaic. With trowel & grout,
he glues tessera to tessera—broken

glass to broken past. He points
to a catacomb maze, invites me
to follow. Descending,

we pass an electrical wire—nerve
of nameless voices, conduit between dead &
living, currents hissing.

Welder of light—teach sparks to chant
antiphonies. Teach the dead to voice
their polyglot exile. Block-by-block,

build a bridge. When a brick implodes
in your hand, you proclaim
its chrism, clay, fire as one entity—ash

scattering.
We are spirit, mind, meat—deceived
into permanence.

No longer formed
or deformed by desire,
I am water reciting its body.

In Her Chapel
La Catedral de Santa Teresa

Avila, Spain

Dean Kostos

She steps from a grotto of ormolu* flames;
Her right hand hovers, blessing, warning.

A torch-like crown sprouts from her scalp;
A honey-fog seethes from her pores

As the chapel breathes,
Breathing out the scent of roses.

Perched on skeletal columns, putti
Whorl clouds from their nostrils.

Bearing Teresa's mortal bones,
A sarcophagous altar sits by her feet.

And the chapel breathes,
Breathing out the scent of roses,

Intoxicating me
Like the spider threading the chandelier.

Tugging her star-sewn mantilla,
Teresa uneclipses her face

And her bird-neck—rising from a nest of frill—
Curves toward me.

Stitched with trumpets formed like mouths
And with scrolls like monkey tails,

Her apron bulges. What does it hold:
A heel of bread, a healing?

The room radiates heat
As if the sun lay buried below the floor,

But I can't move, her mind smelted to mine.
I gulp for air when

Into my lungs the chapel breathes,
Breathing out the scent of roses.

And she gathers this essence to her breasts,
Cradling its invisible bouquet:

Infant version of herself
She again and again gives birth to.

ormolu: alloys used to resemble gold

Away from Dogma

Edward Hirsch

*I was prevented by a sort of shame from going
into churches. . . . Nevertheless, I had three
contacts with Catholicism that really counted.*
—Simone Weil

1. In Portugal

One night in Portugal, alone in a forlorn
village at twilight, escaping her parents,
she saw a full moon baptized on the water
and the infallible heavens stained with clouds.

Vespers at eventide. A ragged procession
of fishermen's wives moving down to the sea,
carrying candles onto the boats, and singing
hymns of heartrending sadness. She thought:

this world is a smudged blue village
at sundown, the happenstance of stumbling
into the sixth canonical hour, discovering
the tawny sails of evening, the afflicted

religion of slaves. She thought: I am
one of those slaves, but I will not kneel
before Him, at least not now, not with
these tormented limbs that torment me still.

God is not manifest in this dusky light
and humiliated flesh: He is not among us.
But still the faith of the fishermen's wives
lifted her toward them, and she thought:

this life is a grave, mysterious moment
of hearing voices by the water and seeing
olive trees stretching out in the dirt,
of accepting the heavens cracked with rain.

2. In Assisi

To stand on the parcel of land where the saint
knelt down and married Lady Poverty, to walk
through the grasses of the Umbrian hills
where he scolded wolves and preached

to doves and jackdaws, where he chanted
canticles to the creatures who share our earth,
praising Brother Sun who rules the day,
Sister Moon who brightens the night.

Brother Fire sleeps in the arms of Sister Water.
Brother Wind kisses Sister Earth so tenderly.
To carry a picnic and eat whatever he ate—
bread and wine, the fare of tourists and saints.

She disliked the Miracles of the Gospels.
She never believed in the mystery of contact,
here below, between a human being and God.
She despised popular tales of apparitions.

But that afternoon in Assisi she wandered
through the abominable Santa Maria degli Angeli
and happened upon a little marvel of Romanesque
purity where St. Francis liked to pray.

She was there a short time when something absolute
and omnivorous, something she neither believed
nor disbelieved, something she understood—
but what was it?—forced her to her knees.

3. At Solesmes

From Palm Sunday to Easter Tuesday,
from Matins to Vespers and beyond, from
each earthly sound that hammered her skull
and entered her bloodstream, from the headaches

she sent into the universe and took back
into her flesh, from the suffering body
to the suffering mind, from the unholy breath
to the memories that never forgot her—

the factory whistle and the branding-iron
of the masters, the sixty-hour work week
and the machine that belched into her face,
the burns that blossomed on her arms—

from whatever weighs us down to whatever
lifts us up, from whatever mutilates us
to whatever spirits us away, from soul
descending to soul arising, moment by moment

she felt the body heaped up and abandoned
in the corner, the skin tasted and devoured;
she felt an invisible hand wavering
over the rags she was leaving behind.

Between the voices chanting and her own recitation,
between the heartbeats transfigured to prayer,
between the word *forsaken* and the word *joy*,
God came down and possessed her.

Rome, *Santa Marie en Cosmedin,* 11/14

Wendy Vardaman

Just inside the portico of this ancient
church built over Greek
ruins at the Forum's edge, grins the pocked
gray Triton face, *Boca de la Veritá,* teeth intact,
through whose oracle mouth visitors insert
a virtue-testing sacrificial wrist. Unwilling to risk
his kiss of truth, its consequence or extra cost, I veer from the line, look
at relics lying under glass instead. *There's Saint*

Valentine's skull, I gasp. The children
resist my attempt to assign
significance to this most unvalentine
like token of a long-moribund
holiday at our house, celebrated back then by cutting
out endless pink hearts, recycled as soon as they looked away:
    flesh, not bone.

St. Peter's Square, 1979

Alan Berecka

College kids half drunk on cheap spumanti,
we decided to stand at the barricades
for hours. As the crowd grew behind us
so did our plan. The new Polish Pope
was returning from Mexico and would pass
within earshot. We knew that he was known
to stop and bless or converse with pilgrims
who spoke his native tongue. The grandson
of Polish immigrants, the group looked to me,
but my vocabulary was bluer than the Pontiff's
eyes. I feared my broken second-hand Polish
was more likely to land me in the bottom
of some secret and dank Vatican dungeon
than it was to gain us a Papal audience.

Plan B, we decided to consult our foreign language
pocket travel guide. Short of receiving the Paraclete's
gift of tongues, phonetics became our only chance.
We leafed through the little Polish it offered, looking
for some phrase that even Americans could pronounce.
Happy with our choice, we practiced in unison
as if we were again pre-communicants chanting
the Baltimore Catechism until we had it right.

That night as the young Pope rode past
a few feet away, we shouted in our best Berlitz,
Where are you going with our baggage?

The passing years bent the Pope
in half and hid him behind a cold
plastic mask, but I still relive that night.
Often in a dream, I see his confused look

snap around to our direction, and I swear
I can hear him answer, *Too far, my son, too far.*

Manhattan

for Robert Creeley

Paul Mariani

Thirty years, and the six-inch scar still there
like a white & leprous flower. Five beers
& five Manhattans at this college bar
in Hempstead & then south with Peers
& Wilbur to the White Castle as I chatter
on about my Ethics test & how Aquinas avers
means can be said to justify the ends (or
is it ends means?) when they're there,
this one in stud leather who insists on star-
ing at my *Manhattan College* jacket. And before
I know it, we're out behind the building, under
the springtime stars, both staggering, stud leather
leering & coming at me, until in sheer terror
I tear into him, fists knotted in his greasy hair,
smashing his head against the blacktop border.
And in two minutes it's over, & through a blur
of cheers I'm downing five Manhattans more,
then swimming upstreet through some phosphor glare
to steal a men's sign for some faceless stranger,
ten feet of coiled barbed wire having so far
stopped him.
          But nothing can stop Manhattan, no sir,
and halfway up the pole razor teeth shear
my leg to lace & then I'm down. And when I pare
back an eyelid the morning after, pain is everywhere,
and there's this ugly fishmouth wound down there,
and I'm tearing past my mother, & at 9:05 I glare
at Ethics Question 1, then down at my bloody cor-
duroys & across at Self-loathing & old friend Fear,

both already bored, & yawning at whatever answer
I come up with for Questions 2 & 3 & 4.

The Cathedral/Basilica of Saint Louis, King of France

Tyler Farrell

All souls in New Orleans are beautiful
when the mist serves us heavenly air
trapped on wet streets, the park noises,
young artists wash feet with a little
fountain water. We crawl along black brick
long cracked streets aimed at the Mississippi.
Fog like smoky faces unbound wishes
humid people, lives eyeing around
the quarter for someone, anyone to tell us
about the parties, the great restaurants,
the crowded bars and discreet strip clubs.
All the rewards complete test and happiness.
If we could live in this parish forever
we could be truly happy our entire lives.

Then a wedding opens chilled cathedral doors
with smells of an ordination at the Vatican.
Grey marble and incense—intoxicates
honors the crowd, union heat throb Christ.
Sounds draw us nearer the ground in reverence
kneeling beneath the sun and crescent moon.
Our minds now unclouded, sins confessed.
Forgiveness is a city of saints, Louis singing
a song for Saint Joseph. He sings also
for the sinners—bourbon street window swingers
bad barkers next to three card monty dealers
near Café Du Monde where a homeless man
hit on me as we sat on black iron benches in the park
with the Civil War cannon, model 1861 parrot rifle.

He said I had real fair skin and I was sweating.
Beignet powdered sugar fell everywhere.
I smiled, listened, chatted with him for a time
about artillery and pirates, about the Jax brewery,
voodoo. Then I went and had a few beers
at the brewery, stumbled back to the Basilica
and with other flaming hearts looked skyward.
We prayed, recited plaque history, visitations
always pondering a pilgrimage to another bar.
Revelation love from local parishioners
indulging the way sinners often indulge.

St. Peter, 1957

Denise K. Lajimodiere

I walk to Safeway helping Sister Genevieve
carry groceries back to the convent,
my braids as blue black as her habit, swishing
back and forth, her rosary beads clicking
like the genuflector cricket during high mass.
I can't speak, she keeps the silence, peering
down at me to keep me in place.
My homemade wool flannel jumper is itchy,
my muslin blouse bleached a ghostly white.

I stay after school,
avoiding the Italian kids calling me squaw,
hurling rocks like bullets.
I receive a scapular from Sister,
and wrap it around my neck
with the others, tucked away under
my ghost shirt.

The Mad Nun

for Alexander Theroux

Dana Gioia

The convent yard seems larger than before
    when late last night he stood a moment
        on Paul's unsteady shoulders

and saw a garden in the moonlight
    full of flowerbeds and orange trees
        around a green-rimmed, empty pond.

Now the paths extend for miles, disappearing
    only in the gloom of trees
        that run along a wall of hedges.

At first the dreamer travels with
    his classmates, but one
        by one they drop away. Paul

transformed into a rosebush when he trips
    on a gardener's shovel. James
        sinks unresistingly into the green

surface of the pond and swims away
    a goldfish. Ernie, whose
        mother warned him when he swore,

steps off the gravel path and blends
    into the ivy, sobbing
        as his hair grows

long and green curling up a tree,
    and slowly the survivor realizes
        that everything growing in this garden

was once a schoolboy—the battered statues,
    the drooping trees, the quiet
        vines climbing up the wall.

Even the spider suspended at the entrance
    of the arbor sits trapped
        like a housefly on his web.

"How do I get out of here?"
    he begs the statues near the pond
        who cannot leave their perpetual

transfixion: Francis in ecstasy
    among the duckweed and beatific
        Dominic who smiles at the bird bath.

But it is always too late.
    A horrible laugh comes
        from behind the Grotto of Our Lady,

and then he knows that the mad nun
    everyone hears about
        has seen him in the garden.

He scrambles down the path, hearing
    her heavy, square-toed shoes
        scuff the ground behind him,

and runs between the hedges—until,
    hidden in the oleander, he hears nothing
        but his own heart beating from exertion

and thinks he has lost her. But suddenly
    he sees a flash of black
        and white behind the bushes.

There is never time to run away
    before her long, white hands
        reach out and shake him

awake, shivering in a damp bed,
　　listening to the rain
　　　　drive nails into the roof,

waiting hours
　　for the humiliating
　　　　light of dawn.

Sainthood

Joseph Bathanti

With apostolic zeal
the nuns made plain that at random
one might be called upon to die for the faith.
Sainthood, they called it, craving
with every breath, they professed,
the opportunity for glory
the headsman occasioned.

I desired sainthood as much as anyone,
but made myself sick obsessing
over what would come for me
at the appointed time, the door
suddenly kicked in by an infidel
demanding I renounce Jesus.

Methods of martyring ranged from simple dispatch—
Venantius was beheaded, Mathias stoned—
to the peevishly imaginative:
Saint James was *hurled down*
from the terrace of the temple
and clubbed to death,
the Forty Holy Martyrs exposed on a frozen pond,
Bartholomew flayed alive.
There were the North American martyrs,
Isaac Jogues and other mad Jesuits,
who suffered fingers and toes chewed off by the Huron.
Still conscious, they watched their organs eaten.

At tiny desks we crayoned
coloring-book sketches of them
in our Catechism Primers,
imagining what kinds of martyrdom

North America would require of us.
Crayola red for blood.
"Stay within the lines," the sisters commanded.

At night, catacombed in bedclothes,
I argued with myself.
Of course I would die for Jesus,
ten days agony, broken glass, snakes,
molten ore, vivisection.
But why not hoodwink my inquisitors?
Simply feed them white lies:
that I was through with Jesus,
I'd worship Baal or Apollo.
To placate them,
to get them to call off the big cats
and put up those blunt rusted instruments.
God would know
that in my heart I hadn't betrayed Him.
Why be tortured and die?
I was only seven.

But, in that same heart, I knew:
Only blood and agony could dye
the royal robes of sainthood;
only death could wear its crown.
There was no *no* when they came for you,
no *yes*. Only death,
and you had to be happy about it.
The martyrs sang praises as they expired.
Further I'd hunker under the covers,
fingering into the bedsheet
the shape of a fish,
then pray to disappear.

In your sleep lions sound like a bed
being dragged across a wooden floor.

The vibrato, ineffable power
gathering breath; and pretty soon
it's inside you. Roaring,
but so much bigger, distant
and large as the ocean,
yet in the house, padding
down the linoleumed hall.

I suppose I got scared and screamed
because my parents would be there,
telling me it was just a dream;
and the three of us would listen
to the lions' caged rumbling.
We lived just two blocks from the Pittsburgh Zoo.
"You've heard them since you were born,"
they reasoned. The way they smiled
at me as if they knew something.
I'd think, maybe finally it's all over.
Maybe I'm in heaven.

Girl Saints

CX Dillhunt

In the orphanage, when I was in fifth grade, I usually put girl saints
about my bed at night—protect yourself, Sister Felicia told us. Put
your
Guardian Angel at the foot of your bed, your Patron Saint at the head,
the rest are up to you, put as many as you like. And on your right and
your left, she advised, put the most powerful.

I knew my mother's favorite saints, my father's too, and I knew all
about St. Lawrence, my patron saint, grilled to death and asking to
be turned over, saying, "I'm done on this side!" As long as I could
remember, I wanted to become a missionary, get tortured, say
something famous, go to heaven.

Sometimes before I finished my saints, I practiced my last line, not
wanting to blow my entrance to heaven, a one-way street for martyrs,
I was told. Burning wouldn't be easy, I thought, but better than
arrows
or crucifixion or stones or lions. I wanted Theresa, but which
one? I had
the same problem with St. Francis. Bilocation—which saint did that?

My Angel at the foot, Lawrence overhead, The Little Flower on the
right. And miracles. I wondered—would I eventually need miracles?
On my left? Claire? Agnes? Bridget? Maria Goretti? What did she
tell her neighbor she wouldn't do before he stabbed her 10, 20, 30, 40
times? Gosh, what was his hurry, why was he so angry?

Who lost their eyes, their boobs and why and how gross to carry
them
out on a tray. OK, for my three miracles: My mother will be cured, my
father will be rich, and grandma will be happy. And for my last
words?

Tomorrow, I always thought, something will come to me. Besides, what

if the Communists take over our country? We all starve to death?

I doubted my last words would count for much.

from *Niagara Falls*

Jim Daniels

25 years ago, in a Detroit church
that's now a gym, I took St. Francis
as my confirmation saint
though Francis was a sissy name.
He talked to animals,
hung out in the woods—
Brother Sun, Sister Moon.

I took that name
and my parents gave me my first watch.
Its band pinched my wrist—
I wasn't ready for that kind of time,
that kind of skeptical attention.

A chart in school kept track
of our memorized prayers. I have forgotten
them all, though I know the beginnings,
little snatches. With a prompter
I could probably make it through.

The Act of Faith, Act of Hope, Act
of Love. The Act of Contrition,
the only one I remember—
" . . . and lead us not into temptation . . . "
The Act of Constriction.

*

Francis the Talking Mule
was the only Francis I ever really knew,
in those old movies with Donald O'Connor
the forerunner to Mr. Ed, the Talking Horse.

I could sing you Mr. Ed's song with no prompting:
A horse is a horse of course of course . . .
What it does for my spirit
I cannot tell you.

I once sent to Hollywood for an autographed
picture of Arnold Ziffle, the pig from *Green Acres*.
More of a piglet. Arnold only grunted
but his owner, Fred, understood Pig—
I like that kind of faith.
Mr. Ed was someone's voice
no miracle: *Oh Wilbur.* Francis
would not have understood you.

*

Last year we lived in Torre Gentile,
a small village a short ride from Assisi.
I had to find out more about
the only name I had ever chosen.
What moved me in Assisi was Cimabue's St. Francis,
not the saintly one in Giotto's frescoes
where he looks too holy and wise to touch,
a religious superman lifting buildings,
casting out demons.

Cimabue's Francis would get his ass kicked
in the gym class locker room. Frail, homely,
big ears. They might call him that—Big Ears,
Dumbo. But he wouldn't be fun to tease—too quiet.
He wouldn't get mad. Maybe he'd even flunk gym
for refusing to box. The kind of kid
you wouldn't mind having sit across
from you in home room. He'd give a kind of comfort
you'd be embarrassed by. *But he's a nice kid*,
you'd say, almost apologetically,
when someone called him a sissy.

*

My oldest friend, Joe, goes to church again
and lifts weights.

His child was born deaf, deformed.
The church helps carry him through.
That, and the weights. He's almost deformed
with muscle, weightlifting magazines
scattered across his basement floor.

I have always been thin
like Joe used to be, though I tried
to gain, to be more substantial—
less wind-blown—more rooted
to the dusty earth.

*

We were altar boys together
till we quit and started going out to eat
at the Clock Pancake House—
Our Lady of the Clock, our first
restaurant. We spent our paper route money.
It was our Mama Anything's.
We didn't know enough then
to read the fine print.

Those pancakes lay heavy in our guts
the sickening sweet syrup
sticking to our fingers.

*

A rosary from the Assisi gift shop
won't heal anyone, Joe, nor will the muscles
you've built up. But maybe they will bring
a little peace, clear peace with no interference,

no background noise. A little peace here, now,
like when we walked through the winter dark
to serve at morning mass, the streets
quiet, headlights sifting through the falling snow.

Maybe we could've simply turned around
and walked home then, blessed by the walk,
blessed by the holy frozen waters,
the snow falling on us,
without going in to the cruets and chalice,
our memorized prayers and stiff knees.

*

A little peace, a good thing. A little
humility, the last word of Francis's prayer,
"Canticle of the Creatures." It moves me—
how else to say it?

Joe, what can we give each other but solace?
Here, let me offer up a dark snowy morning
before the world wakes up.

Saint Valentine's Dinner with Nuns

Annette Spaulding-Convy

In the refectory, I light Sacred Heart
    of Jesus candles, place a neon-pink carnation
    and a Hershey's Kiss on each plate.

My Shirley Temple spiked
    with sacramental wine, I hang a cardboard Cupid
    around Saint Dominic's neck,

then scatter red confetti on the oak table,
    making love
    look like something from a second grade classroom,

something as virginal as our white dresses.
    For the centerpiece, there's the dime-store
    statue of *The Ecstasy of Saint Teresa*,

that angel jabbing his long spear
    into her breast,
    God's way of saying, *be mine, sweetie-pie,*

luv u, hot stuff—
    Conversation Hearts
    spill like fire into our empty laps.

All Hallow's Eve

Joseph Bathanti

Dressed as our patron saints,
we entered the convent through its scullery:
stainless steel, white vaults, vessels
dangling from black hooks.

Then into the marble corridor,
off which the sick chamber bore,
where we cowed, attendant to the next
click of Sister Daria's fingers.

The walls respirated with vespers.
Camphor escaped the jamb beyond
which Sister Clement was dying.
Her room was overheated,

the curtain thrown back
to let through the soaped window
the end of the day's gray light.
At the headboard

stood an orange air-cylinder.
Wearing a blue robe, hands braided
with a tiny-beaded pink rosary,
its Christ silver on a pink cross,

the ancient nun angled into a mound
of bedclothes. No wimple, but a thin
veil pinned to her head, faded gray
hair misted at her temples.

Prodded by Daria, as we paraded
around the bed, we one at a time
approached Sister Clement:
Stephen, Joan, Christopher, Paul,

on and on, an entire roll of martyrs,
tortured, dead in droves, without complaint.
At each proclamation, she smiled
and nudged sweets across the spread.

When I stepped up and whispered,
Joseph, she dug her hand in mine
and sighed until she moaned.
I had disguised myself as a just man.

Had we been alone, I might have asked
to touch her hair, confessed
I'd been thinking only of the shoplifted
Tareytons I'd smoke that night vampiring

through the streets. I might have cried,
Instead, with the lump of chocolate
she'd stuck in my fist, I spun,
suddenly nauseated at the room's red heat

and my horsehair beard. Thrashing
with my staff through my fellow saints
I rushed into the convent garden.
In the house across the avenue,

the whores were just waking,
goblins already on their porch,
trick or treating.
Chocolate dripped from my hand.

The Feast of St. Anthony

Gerry LaFemina

Patron Saint of Padua & of my mother,
finder of lost objects, there you are
held aloft by men, bearing you south
in effigy along Mulberry Street
while tourists click snapshots & spill
powdered sugar from zeppole
on their shirts. So many things I've lost
I can't pray for—those foolish
abstractions of innocence & faith; the items
I no longer care about like those model
planes that flew into the Bermuda triangle
of my parents' separation . . . .
What benediction should I seek?
Everyone seems to be having the good
time they were searching for, wheels of chance
spinning & the Sons of Garibaldi Marching
Band playing behind you. I never knew
that cheering is a type of prayer.
The grandfathers clap & count the money
as the Nonis weep with old loss.
Because you carry the infant Jesus
resplendent against the simple
folds of your Franciscan frock
the littlest kids run up to you to pin
another five dollar bill at your feet.

The Patron Saint
of Lost and Found

Greg Kosmicki

One time in 5th grade I lost my Catechism
so I looked in all the usual places—

under the davenport, under my bed, on the closet floor
stuffed full as usual with all the junk
I cleaned up for the last weeks,
the clothes hamper, the shelf in my room,
under the seats in the cars,
under the kitchen table,
even in my desk.

Nowhere was it to be found.
After a week or so I gave up hope
and started to pray to some Saint
who's the Patron Saint of Lost and Found
or Lost Causes or something like that,
and after a week or so
not really having given up on the Saint
I went and bought another Catechism
because the teacher was bugging me
and I had a lot of stuff to memorize out of it.
The day after I bought the Catechism
like mom made me with my own money
("You won't forget that way, Honey,")
I looked down at my feet while waiting
so we could go to school
in the back seat of the station wagon
and saw the missing Catechism.
I couldn't believe my eyes!

I never told anybody about praying
to that Saint
because it was, after all, 1959.

I would have never brought it up even now
if I hadn't been rummaging around
like in an old closet full of toys
through the clutter in my head
where the Saint whose name I have long since lost
stayed, and searched, and found this poem for me.

Saint Anthony's Day

for SMB

Charlotte Barr

*We beg you . . . that the soul may safely flee to you on that
last day of affliction and fire, when the silver rope will be
broken.*

—St. Anthony of Padua

Ecce quam bonum et quam jucúndum habitare fratres in unum.

—Psalm 132

June thirteenth, my erstwhile feast comes round again,
And the anniversary day of my perpetual vows.
I was twenty-three; in the certitude that youth allows,
I said, "for all my life," and sure I meant it then.

St. Anthony doesn't reproach me, stays my friend,
And some companions keep my memory.
Today I think of them and celebrate what has been,
How good and pleasant still that story.

The American Cathedral

Alan Berecka

Young Staples aspired to fame and piety,
to become the American Padre Pio.
He too would dress in brown woolen robes,
and, God willing, he would learn to hear
silent confessions, hover above the altar
during high mass, allow his spirit to travel
as he slept to comfort souls darkened by doubt,
but mostly he wished to heal the sick with hands
that God would pierce with fragrant wounds.

But his years in the pulpit only brought
Young Staples to middle age, so he decided
to trade in Jesus Christ for Adam Smith,
Catholicism for capitalism, middlemen
for buying wholesale-direct. He renounced
his vows and fell in bed then love with an earthy
woman. He began to preach a new brand
of Good News. Each Sunday he promises his flock
everything in glossy ads found between the comics
and the classifieds, and his disciples come
in great numbers, believing that their problems
can be solved by shopping in the city
of Corpus Christi at the Padre Staples Mall.

The Thursday Collection

Sts. Anne and Joachim Church,

Fargo

Timothy Murphy

Thanksgiving was frozen and gray.
Three thousand dollars and change
were donated at our Masses,
and our pastor was moved to arrange
a gift for Dorothy Day,
a thousand three dollar dinners
for the battered, the drunkards, the sinners.
She cares for each person who passes
addicted, alone or astray,
and ours are the souls she would save
as we try to rise out of the grave.

The Saint Vincent de Paul Food Pantry Stomp

Madison, Wisconsin, 1980

Martín Espada

Waiting for the carton of food
given with Christian suspicion
even to agency-certified charity cases
like me,
thin and brittle
as uncooked linguini,
anticipating the factory-damaged cans
of tomato soup, beets, three-bean salad
in a welfare cornucopia,
I spotted a squashed dollar bill
on the floor, and with
a Saint Vincent de Paul food pantry stomp
pinned it under my sneaker,
tied my laces meticulously,
and stuffed the bill in my sock
like a smuggler of diamonds,
all beneath the plaster statue wingspan
of Saint Vinnie,
who was unaware
of the dance
named in his honor
by a maraca shaker
in the salsa band
of the unemployed.

The Voodoo Doll Parade

Lauren Schmidt

When the man outside the liquor store collapsed
like a denim sack, when he wailed and moaned,
recited the Hail Mary, lying on his back,
when he grabbed his gut, kicked his legs
as if running fire out of them,

I knew he was one of us.

I knew that some lover had his likeness
in her hands, "You Oughta Know"
blaring from her stereo. In her room,
the blended stench of nachos, margaritas,
and acetone. A cleansing mask swooped
around her T-zone into a wicked, jokered grin.

I knew just how she made his twin:

First, two sticks tied, an ice-pop crucifix.
Spanish moss twined into muscles
and limbs. Canvas pulled and stitched.
Next, she sewed Xs for eyes like a cartoon
drunk from a bottle marked *skull & crossbones*,
his lips inked in a slivery smile.
She left him naked, drew pecs like saggy breasts,
squiggly lines out from which limps a shriveled dick,
a pair of balls with eyes and a frowny-face.

When he whirled to his side, I knew

that meant she tossed him to her girlfriend
who stabbed him through the head.
Passed again, another takes her turn,

peppering small holes over his chest
before driving it up into the forlorn sack.

At last the sirens arrived: a stake driven
in his backbone. His jaw unhinged,
tongue sagged from his mouth,
a chewed and bloody strip of bacon.
Bottles of beer rolled from his bag like exotic women.

Yes, he's one of us now. He will be in line tonight.
At first, he'll be looking for the floats and dancers,
the barbershop quartets. He'll be wondering where
the banners might be, the beauty queens
waving from the shoulders of Chevrolets.
But it's just us, like him, figuring,
Who would have put me here?

At midnight the marching will begin.
We'll sprout their pins like urchins of the sea;
we'll be their barbed St. Sebastians,
their Christmas-bulbed trees;
their maps of waged war, their holiday destinations;
bull's-eyes in dive bars staggered with hits.

We'll all wince in the ills they inflict upon us,
and no one's unasked for, or ever allowed to leave.

Such defenseless skin. Wisps of silver spring
from our hearts, our spines, our Xs for eyes
while inside, our human stitch unravels.

Another Mary

Laurie Byro

I was afraid of sleeping so close to where my granny told me
the pineys lived. They pinched babies and had red eyes.
If you were raised on these stories, you believed. My belly

big with cowardice and fear, I hitchhiked to the Black Horse
Pike and got a ride all the way from Absecon to Atlantic City.
Our baby was born cold and white as the marble statues

I prayed before. On the beach, the ocean folds and falls.
One white candle hosts this miracle, shines and shines.
Competes with stars. I meet a new friend, while I am squatting

like an Indian, passing afterbirth and keening at the moon.
He is younger than me, a man with ruddy cheeks and old
track marks, and I say Halleluiah perhaps he would warm

my backside until the right one came along.
But we got separated somehow, I kept sleeping under
the boards until I got up the nerve to try the woman's shelter

on Baltic and Mediterranean Avenues. I kissed Martha through
the cell bars when I got caught stealing groceries
and when her pimp got us both out, I figured it was a sign

from God and I should think about calling my folks and ask
if I could come back home. But then I found him poking through
the dumpster outside of that casino, and we could make

a feast on the fat gamblers' leavings. He remembered right away
that my belly was flat and he'd promised me a present when
we were crying on the beach. We went into an all night

deli that sold rolls, pastrami and notions. He paid for some bread
and I put two skeins of wool under my coat. We sat on a picnic
bench and snow scuttled sideways like crabs. I knit him

a scarf and some fingerless gloves. If luck was with us,
we would find a warm corner under the boardwalk to sleep
and in the morning when all those white candles I had lit

outside our wooden cave went out and cold stars fell around
the statue of the mother in the courtyard, I would begin
a blanket to leave around her marble skin to warm that baby up.

All Saints Day

Kevin Brown

Perhaps St. Matthew's columns
always came out correctly,
but he struggled with dangling
modifiers and comma splices;
and St. Christopher could
supposedly find his way anywhere
on the Appian Way, but whenever
he was asked for directions, he
reversed right and left, leading

many listeners to end up in
Brundisium instead of Capua;
and while St. John Frances Regis
might have blessed many unions,
he never remembered to take
out the trash. St. Gregory the
Great struggled with self-esteem,
and, while St. Francis fed the
animals, both physically and

spiritually, children who were
found underfoot were forced
away more harshly than was
necessary. Whether they bit
their nails or struggled with
sloth, envy, or anger, among
others, saints are easier to see
at a distance, not when we live
with them day after day after

day, when we have to see their
holiness through their humanity.

So, on this day, let us look past
what we lack—my manners and tact
that lead to awkward social situations
or your acquiescence to those you
love until it is turned against you—
see the sacred in others, believe
we can all be saints one day.

III.

Sickness and Death

St. Agnes, Pink-Slipped

Ann Cefola

Hospital changes name to Westchester Medical Center, White Plains Pavilion.

—*May 2003*

Walking past forsythia, magnolia, dogwood, over the soft bed of
   cherry blossoms shed,
she wonders if this is what she most wanted to avoid:
   the consolation of angels.

Did you see her hitching along North Street? Melted halo liquid
   light around her neck,
once golden raiment a yellow raincoat, hovering toes now firmly
   bound in sneakers.
     Recalling newborns

she coaxed into sterile birth room light; children, bald, bleeding,
   incubated,
who healed at her radiant grin, the aged whose trembling hands
   she'd grasp,
     telling them: *Heaven! Imagine!*

And they: *Okay, my last breath.* Then *No, please another look.*
Finally, their resigned: *Let's go.*
     Thinking about that envelope

left by the CEO. Some younger nurses wept and Colombian
   gardeners crossed themselves, muttering, *¡Dios mío!* before deli-
   cately removing her statues throughout the grounds.
     Interceding on her own behalf,

she asks for work as a home health aide, local apparition or might
   she replace

a negligent guardian angel? Anything not to lose the perfume of
     seasons,
          like the lilac she brushes

her wet face against, the very air she breathes a vibrant green
     vapor,
and tulips her eyes widen to take in
          like the holiest red and gold robes.

Now she understands the dilemma of the dying: how they don't
     want to turn
their backs on the sun-edged bloom, how one human spring
          can ruin paradise.

Portrait of Mr. Menzies as St. Rita of Cascia

Susan L. Miller

After his stroke, for months, all I hear
of Mr. Menzies are stories his daughter carries
from the assisted living: he's improving,

he uses the wheelchair adeptly, he's ready
to return home. Then for a month, requests
for the priest. I write and mail letters, send him

prayer-cards of St. Francis, joke about my forays
into the lectorship, the Sunday I make everyone
do extra penance by reading the wrong section.

Finally, one Sunday I hear he's confessed
and received communion, and two weeks
later he's sitting in the pew, the back

of his head familiar, though shorn of
the small ponytail he used to wear. I gaze
through the homily at his curls of white hair.

When he rises for the Eucharist, returning
at once to his seat, I see his face in profile, skin
of his jaw translucent, veins visible under

his tan. A hard lump rises into my throat; I'm
so choked I worry I can't swallow the host.
But after the Mass, he greets me: "Thank you

for remembering me," he says, supported by
a three-footed cane. He asks about the bandage
on my ankle. "In case of a sprain, you chill

a quart bottle. Roll it over the ankle to make
the tendons return to their right places.
Then you tear a paper grocery bag in strips.

Soak them in vinegar, and wrap the foot. This
will bring the swelling down." I smile, remembering
the cough remedy he'd offered the week

I was baptized: coconut oil, lime juice, and salt,
which I warmed in a shot glass and drank.
Disgusting, but it worked. I thank him,

and we walk out together, me limping slightly,
him, tall and graceful in his good grey suit,
his cane barely grazing the floor.

The Lives of the Saints

Suzanne Paola

When I first learned about atoms in high school
nothing seemed more ridiculous than life
if that's all it was: tiny, disintegrating, empty, all-the-same.
Dustdots streaming
toward an even larger collapse.
Everywhere. My mother in her pinkchecked party apron
spun in bits to the dining room, a duck nucleused
by *Joy of Cooking* sauce l'orange in her arms.

& my lubehaired dad crisping the *Tribune* down
to come to her.
He was something else totally,
really just a bundle of nervous hoops.

He knew my mother as small
already, the TV
blaring *I love ya little cutie but the office is my duty*
as legions of husbands left their wives onscreen.

What I saw kept showing me
its rounding Ferris wheels of movement, its poor parts.

At Mary Star of the Sea High School, 5th period science class
it got hard to believe in anything, seeing it all
as the same at the root—
one or two dots' difference, carbon's diamond,
or bound with other, almost identical
atoms, it's me.

Then 7th period Religion we read about
the lives of the saints, so it was like
hearing them try to yank the absurdity to something else.

Or maybe the saints knew it
too, Catherine
with her puslicking, her meals of vomiting & celery.

I loved those people & their comic gestures.
Rose of Lima rubbing pepper on her skin, Jerome
turning restlessly on his nails
showed their indifference to the state of matter.

They were the first atomic scientists.
Francis' parents
cast him off, Rose's too, saints blew up
the world around them.
Like they had to start that way, freed electrons,
so the way in front of them could be clear.

Later I saw them all the time
when my mother grew their look.
I say *grew*. It emerged, a new life, from her face.
The one where you smile & it's real
but the rest of your face does something else completely.

Looks beyond the room, your eyes heavy
with the weight of two existences.

It seemed my mother's cancer hungered for her eyes.
A soft round on the ovary, larger than the organ
it consumed.

They took out everything, the first plushed bed
of my babyhood. "All gone," says my mother
then tells me how she bled, "like
saffron threads" (Indian cooking
with Craig Claiborne, a phase of hers).

She took to eating bacon & eggs & liver.
She's had her thyroid & appendix removed

& tells me she feels like a bladder or balloon, a skin
clung to a wind that's blowing her clean.

After chemo I set her hair the way she likes it, the strands
cytoxin didn't gobble up.
I trapped them in pink rollers the size of fingers—she used them
on me a few times—they had little spikes all around,

& she'd emerge re-done, scrollheaded,
a fountain of those Jewish scripture-curls.

For a while I couldn't justify my love of sweets
with all I knew of the world, it stung
or spun, Catherine
lived years on the Host, & I
took a cake-decorating class and squeezed the icing bag straight
    into my mouth.
It saved me: the frosting
mostly powdered sugar, only heaps of sugar
can make a good form & keep it.
Flavors like chocolate just a whisper of elseness

& my secret love became that sugarshock
of icing, that knock to the jaw,
your tongue & teeth can actually vibrate from it.
Your mind screams *pleasure*
your teeth hit with that corruption nervescream *hurt*.

I made cakes & brought them to my mother
first her favorite flowers like roses & bleeding hearts
then drip bags, syringes, & whatever
they took out of her, I made.
I even made a sheetcake using fondant to mold
the smug, sporebearded face of an oncologist she couldn't stand.

She couldn't eat them & I didn't want her to.
It was a way of seeing her life as holdable, slapstick, nothing
but the sweet inside.

San Rocco

Joseph Bathanti

In the rainy spring of 1919,
my grandmother, pregnant with my mother,
was infected with influenza.
To the headboard of her sickbed,
my grandfather nailed an icon of San Rocco,
protector against plague and contagions.

Bearded, in a striped pilgrim robe hitched above
the thigh sored with sooty legions
contracted curing peasants of Black Plague
simply by making over them the Sign of the Cross,
young Rocco points to his wounds.
On his left breast blazes
a red cross-shaped birthmark.

My grandmother wore like martyr's rags her horrid fever.
She hadn't eaten in five days.
The baby, in its sterile cave, kept perfectly still.
My grandfather knelt, praying for a miracle;
he'd later testify he remembered nothing.

Utmost delirium often conjures,
among the faithful, benefactors:
the Mother of God;
a sly angel ancestor hovering
in the ether above the house;
apparitions summoned
by the sick's yearning to be well.

Yet the story remains.
My mother, then unborn, now 85,
branded at birth with the red cross on her breast too,

swears to it:
Rocco walked up the stairs from the kitchen
with a warm loaf of bread;
my grandmother rose instantly and ate—
my grandfather, still and gossamer, hands vespered
on the quilt, as if suspended in photogravure.

Then my grandmother, the baby jiggling
like a jubilant spider in her womb, and Rocco,
in the silent bedroom smoky with twilight,
danced like gypsies the Tarantella;
prancing clockwise, hands flicking
bird-like above their heads.

A blue astringent light,
like the one that emanated from Rocco's body at death,
murmured over them, burning
blue the amnion where my mother
finally opened her eyes and prepared
for her long descent into the world
as music, a mandolin, suddenly issued
from the Benvenutos across the alley,
where their youngest child, Vito,
near dead with flu as well,
was also visited at that exact moment by San Rocco.

That evening, the night of my mother's birth,
every infected soul on Omega Street was healed.

Watching You, Mother, Almost Thanksgiving, St. Jude's I.C.U.

Susanna Rich

What's this? you ask of your mother's
ruby signet ring on my finger. *Pretty,*
you say, pulling it toward you,

fading to sleep.
Can't rouse, can't leave you.
Sit, nibbling on my nails

bitter from your disinfectant.
Sixty sweeps of the red clock hand,
overhead vents throbbing

from a distant generator . . .
this is how it's been—
me watching you

in the sleep of your life . . .
Jerk—your right leg jerks up—
knee waving like a cat's tail.

Hands clutch and unclutch.
Fingers wagging.
What cell memory wills

your ninety-year-old body
to St. Vitus a dance you didn't
dance? To shadow box

what cause you didn't square?
Conduct what concert of yourself?
You who had only your flight

from Budapest, Christmas angels,
rides in a white Tempest to give me . . .
I've slipped on this family crest

fashioned in someone else's birthstone—
this ring you waved between me
and my husband, until you slipped it

from your finger at Windows on the World.
What more must I do for you to come to
me? Oh, St. Jude, Patron of the Impossible,

Man of the Last Moment—
come, sit with me. I have become
my mother's mother

holding vigil over her little girl—
my mother unfinished—
longing to awaken.

Bernadette in Transit

Mary Ann Samyn

First glance: mistook her for Mary.

Who could tell? One good eye,
chipped, just a bit of iris.

Weren't Mary's eyes always blue on the cover of the
missalette?

Bernadette's too, apparently.

Nearby: St. Peter on his rock.
Nearby: Christ, reclining, scary-lifesize.
Nearby: His Sacred Heart, Sacré Coeur protruding
from a banner, three nice drops of his embroidered blood . . .

—Bush Antiques, New Orleans

Meanwhile, on the edge of town . . .
Meanwhile, long ago . . .
My mother came, by bus, to this place,
to a space apart.

Meanwhile, from B's left arm
a wire protruding where her hand
was attached, once, where she held
what—?

—And me thinking, *how might I use her?*
Practical. Mercenary.
Or, more ominously, *how am I like her?*
Or, just, *what is her provenance?*
What's my good reason?

But not thinking of my mother
who stayed at the edge of town,
who suffered
as cheaply as possible.

Bernadette = $95: discount plunder
shipping & handling = $80

I flinch a bit. ka-ching!

—But what sound does a saint make?
(This thought occurred.)
Original energy, sure, her throat, God's—,
no doubt.

But what about a saint in a box?

Somewhere, the UPS man listens
as I will soon: her three red streaks
(left breast. spray paint? not quite, too
careful.), go high-pitched and electrical.

More and more, my mother had experiences alone.
She did nothing that I know of.

Likewise, I keep quiet.

Bernadette has a number: 16242.
She has a location and a routing
I can follow if I want.

About her I know nothing, nothing.
Then 18 visions of "call me
the Immaculate Conception,"
and the necessary testimony.

This was Lourdes.

Before the *then* of it got to be too much,
and she went back to cholera, so common:
"acute, often fatal . . . characterized by . . .
blah blah blah . . . and collapse."

Later, sainthood. Later, her incorruptible body:
three times exhumed: with a sweet odor and
"completely victorious over the laws of nature."

The statue, however, is in its own collapse:
paint chips along the folds of her dress and veil.

What she's been through—

Now is a funny word,
meaning, as it can, my mother
remembering she was fine alone.
Or also, me, a little later,
my reaction—

> My worries are typical
> and ridiculous—*has she been*
> *jostled much? has she*
> *cried out?*—though she is a saint,
> she is in a good box.

The receipt arrives. Bernadette to follow.
But snow fills the garden, the space I planned:
some white, some darkening . . . as around
her eyes, her photo readily available:

so *this is what a saint looks like* (half *oh*—,
half *yeah*—)

. . . *this is the white veil, the*—

—Compassion, occasionally,
sure. Spurred on—
by what she's been through,
the look—I recognize it:
the photo of her, age 14:
dark hair, folded hands:

earnestness + ferocity . . .

O God, protector of the humble,
grant that I may—

. . . and be deserving of—

—And if it were possible
could she be among
the cured?

O patroness of the sick—

The instructions say: *inspect this.*
The crown of her head (no crown
though; just cold) peeks out
from among the packing peanuts.

This is arrival—I am thrilled.

This is safety.

My mother, however, remains
elsewhere, meanwhile.

An unsafe box.

A box of waiting.

A box of *not now, dear*—

Shopping for Miracles: Lourdes, 1979

Alan Berecka

Looking for a cheap souvenir, I browsed
the curio shops. Deciding against frisbees
stamped with Mary or t-shirts picturing
the sainted Bernadette, I opted
for a convertible virgin, a plastic bottle
with a threaded neck and screw-top head.
Pleased with the absurdity of my purchase,
I walked to the shrine, past the grotto
and its glass-encased stream. I waded
through the tides of the sick and dying
to a brass tap where I filled my Mary
to her Adam's apple—half hoping the water
might cure my bed-bound mother.

Exiting the grounds, I passed bazooka-sized
votives and eyed the infirm. I noticed
that the ill seemed to suffer most from aging.
Confused, I began to question our shared faith—
*Everyone wants to meet Jesus, but nobody
wants to die*—the old adage come to life. I grew
tired to my marrow. I saw a rusted garbage bin
and decided to can my plastic Queen of Heaven,
but when I lifted the tin lid, there on top
of the trash sat a broken wooden cane.

I returned to the States with a glass flask
filled with holy water which I gave
to my mother who accepted the gift
with gratitude, although she remained

bedridden and continued to say the rosary through her pain every day until she died.

The Priesthood

Mary Jane Nealon

I.

I thought I'd be a priest
or an Indian Saint like Kateri Tekawitha—
she survived smallpox with blinded eyes and a disfigured face.
The book about her was the first thing I stole.

I took a chunk of fudge and gave it to my brother.
I wanted to be *heroic*. Caught,
I was forced to tell Father Griffith, but in the confessional,
I wanted to be the powerful one, not the sinner on the other side.
I made a private vow.

Pope Paul the VI appeared on the steps of St. Pat's.
The crowd screened, swooned.
Blessings flew in the air. I thought I was seeing Jesus
and nearly fainted from hysteria.
My mother pointed to the Pope,
He's just a priest, she said, to calm me.

I wanted to be a priest: person in charge of ceremony,
magician of body and blood,
absolver of thieves like me.

My brother discovered a tumor. *Grapefruit*
they said. As though a tangy comparison could calm us.
I stole many things that year: the useless scapula
on my brother's bedpost. Fishnet stockings.
A change purse: small and green and leather
with a hammered rose. My stealing embarrassed the family.

Every Wednesday I was sent to after-school confession
for bad kids and adulterous wives. My priest idols

tilted their heads towards me,
whispering delicious forgivenesses.
Remember, my mother told me, *a priest is just a man.*

When my brother was nineteen, God suddenly swirled
in the invisible, an *idea.*
My mother's hand lingered on my back at my brother's deathbed.
She turned away from the final moment.
Everyone but us in the hallway when the clotted blood left his
    pelvis,
flew from the nest of his beloved lower belly,
and traveled to his heart. There in the room above the river,
he stared at me, breathless and afraid. His ribs,
like the hull of a boat, bowed out. And I in my fantasy
laid my hand on his forehead and told him how to go.
Convinced him of the way to go. Blessed him with my secret
priestness. Between us, the idea of God took shape.
This skin-to-skin pressure in the face of death's fluent body.
My mother's hand to my back while she looked out the window.

II.

Before my mother died
she lifted her arm so fast
she hit me in the face.
She was trying to *throw* her arms around me,
did throw them,
heavy as they were for her
who could no longer lift them.

When she did die, at 3 in the morning, I had fallen asleep,
my head on her knees, her hand on my head.
All the others were in their rooms, restless or dreaming.
I woke to her breath giving out, woke to her hands reclaiming my
    brother,
to her turning back from the window in the room where he had
    died,

turning finally to face him. And I left them there.
My hand on his forehead, her hand on my hair.
I am a keeper of things that don't belong to me.

The truth is, the Jesuits brought smallpox to the Indians.
They brought the need for conversion: fear
in the face of the epidemic. And Kateri Tekawitha,
scarred and made unbeautiful, wanted to be near them. Knew
that they would touch her, as they touched all the disfigured
and unpure, just as I knew
that the clap of the priest's incense holder released more
than the musky scent of God.

The Maculardegeneration Boogie

a story from The Lives of the Saints, Blind Edition

Jim Daniels

My mother, bad magician,
mad scientist, limping dancer,
blind juggler in the kitchen,
dips her fingers into measuring cups,
traces the S and P on the shakers,
waits for the dough to rise
in the broiler, the dials spinning counter-
blind-wise, the oven still stinging
with burn-off from last week's erupting lasagna
and hot cross buns turned to holy rocks
to stone St. Lucy, the patron saint
of blindness.

St. Lucy carries her eyes on a plate
like a server of hors d'oeuvres
at a wedding reception. My blind mother
would ask, *what are these?*
or maybe just pop one in her mouth
and be surprised.

She has found surprise
to be overrated, she who always
loved the mad tingle of the un-
expected, her open-mouthed
laughter spreading like heat
from the open oven.

It's as if she carved all her recipes
into a bar of soap, then washed her hands.
She limps back and forth

to the buzzing of the giant
Martian timer, cruel, untranslatable.

She's stubborn as any martyr
with faith in both God
and not dying, not curling
into herself like a poisoned worm
in her special chair cushioned
against the steel rods in her back.

She cooks. Is cooking.
Continues to cook. My father lurks
with the fire extinguisher.
She cuts him a piece of cake
in the shape of the state of
Oklahoma? West Virginia?
He shuts up and eats it.
He tells her it is good.
She made him sick last week.

When he tries to help, the air burns
like melted plastic on the wrong burner.
I remember the pattern of her pinched crusts,
perfect waves lapping against the edges.
Now it's, man the lifeboats.
She's bent over, the knife just inches
from her nose. Her hip's shot.
Her life cooked. Her rosary lost.

She tried to get the dough to rise
in winter sun streaming in
but even the sun's turning against her,
despite her special orange glasses
and wide-brimmed hat, a desperado
waiting for her cue but no one's
giving her a clue. The timer erupts again

or the smoke alarm or the telephone
with its mysterious disappearing numbers.

I'm sure you have a lot of advice for us.
Leave a phone message.
They never check the machine.
My father's going to get a red flag
to tie to her walker so when summer
comes she can limp across the street
to the store where they know her well enough
to take her list and walk her down the aisles.

She listens to a book on tape. *Her* eyes
on a plate. Dinner ready soon.
Hungry yet?

Elegy for a Living Man

for Theodore, with Parkinson's disease

Dean Kostos

While waves thrashed in the distance,
my father's body hardened into a pillar of salt.

Shadow-shafts spoked from the base,
shifted like clock hands, ticking away sun.

Voices crowded his skull with pleas;
his crippled lips couldn't answer.

When feathery shadows erased his dust-scrawled names
(lawyer, politician, speaker),

darkness consumed his room.
Like a pair of egrets, his moonpolished eyes

fluttered to a replica of our family—
molded by him, preserved in a jar of brine.

Flinching, his eyes returned to socket-
caves, numbed into sleep:

Regrets flocked from nightmare-swamps,
beating wings and beaks against the glass

as though starving, and his body
a mound of dying fish.

A specter of the man he'd hoped to be
slid from his side, passed through the glass

to battle the beasts like Saint George
with a sword that severs past from present.

The assault muted the squawks:
RECALL? RECALL? RECALL? . . .

Sun sliced the horizon. The regrets scattered,
blood splattered on question-mark necks.

A few feathers quivered on the panes.
Dad opened his eyes as I

wrestled him into his wheelchair.
Screeching along the carpet,

the wheels' spokes, like antennas, flashed
with the static of things unspoken.

From his tongue's cocoon, words flitted:
"Uh-yee nayveur woonteed hoort-oort yeeou . . . "

Cupped in prayerful gesture, his hands filled with
something unseen which he tendered

to friends long dead, his mother, his father.
"Oo-whyy woor they-ee heeyere?"

He swatted the air, besieged
by insects with human heads.

Blued by TV's flicker, he curved into his wheelchair,
eyes dazing:

From his tracheotomy-hole,
an iridescent weave of lightning

rushed up in the form of a dancer, free
to move, to loosen sinew and bone.

The dancer spun, coaxing him: *Let me go.*
When its spinning churned the carpet to sand,

Dad and I sat on the beach again.
I pressed my face to the grainy warmth:

Like a brave listening for hoofbeats, I
heard a heartbeat and plunged in my hands,

wrenching out an infant heart.
I rescued it from a strangle of roots,

secured the pounding bulb with toothpicks
above a jar of tears,

and placed it on a ledge near the ocean
which sputtered his name, his *nay me*:

The ore adored
He the ardor the odor the O-door

Theodore

His Mouth

Lois Marie Harrod

Those last six days
even the smile disappeared
and his mouth became the sink hole
I had been pushed back from as a child,
a weak spot where the earth gave way.

But the mouth did not give way.

It stretched itself
into the outline of a rotting pear,
a slack rubber band,
as if he were holding the left
side open for a last word
while the right lay too feeble to listen.

And all the while I could hear his voice
pleading from the speechless pulpit
cannot you wait with me one hour.

Of course, that too was understated
as his life had been. A man can live
without praise, and now he was
living without water. Three, four,
five, six days his Gethsemane continued,
dying as he had dictated
without intervention.

Six days with his breath
so soiled my sister and I
held wet towels to our faces
when our mother was not watching.

I understood then how those
who died without odor
could be considered saints,
bodies incorruptible,
but not how my mother
could say she smelled
nothing at all.

Swans in Flight

Christine Redman-Waldeyer

Near the entrance I imagined Saint Peter
weighing your good deeds with your bad;

where did the anchor lay of your sexuality?
Inscribed on your headstone with a valley

of lines that make up the letters and numbers
is your name stamped into the granite,

is a pronouncement of your short life
into the gray stone.

I can remember Point Pleasant boardwalk,
how you dared me to the Ferris Wheel-like ride

that locked us into a cage
spun us and held us upside down.

I closed my eyes through that entire ride.
Then I never imagined the need to borrow

a dress for your funeral,
for the good-bye we never had

because of the distance that had grown between us.
There are times when I think of you;

they are usually at night when the ocean can be
heard from my bedroom,

or when the honking of geese in flight
is just over the rooftops,

but more often it is when I pass the lake,
and catch the lone Swan take flight.

She is that question I ask myself over and over.
Did St. Peter let you in?

I imagine her invitation to climb onto her back
so I can find you;

when I do,
you are standing just outside the gates

alone like a shirt I found on a sale rack
that hasn't got a tag:

The cashier much like St. Peter is confused.
He is scanning the bar code,

calling for help over the intercom.
My Swan takes me back to the edge of the water.

I do not risk following her to her nest,
because she like the question hisses now,

warns me away.
Still I love her though she has turned on me;

I love her for her slender out-stretched neck,
for her flight in motion.

Halo

for Katharine

Jennifer Bates

Last spring, you dreamed yourself a saint,
another Catherine broken on the wheel.
Living on water and delusion,
you nourished yourself with portraits
of martyrs in the local museum.
You ran without purpose or ceasing
like some rat in an experimenter's maze
until the depression gripped you,
forcing you down on your knees.

Locked in your frantic cycle,
you tried to escape your body for good.
You fed yourself the bitter food
of fifty sedatives and went to sleep.
Waking to doctors in a white room,
you couldn't believe you had risen
to the light of one more day.
To you, that room is a second prison
you must somehow try to escape.

Where you are now was once all farms.
Instead of the bony hospital, perhaps
a huge barn rested its dusty frame.
Bathed in a cloud of chaff and dim light,
the oxen trod their inevitable path
around and around the open floor.
Their iron feet beat a circle in place,
and their haunches moved like giant wheels,
groaning beneath their bodies' weight.

The oxen have all disappeared.
And still, in your sleep, you hear
the thudding. Does it comfort you,
who can only travel the circle
you pace in your small white room?
You are pacing it now, my broken saint,
with the air around your head
beaten tighter than gold, and your face
turned in shadow like the moon.

Rose-Flavored Ice Cream with Tart Cherries

Kraków, Poland

Karen Kovacik

The June air's woozy with unshed rain.
Even the Baroque saints look hot,
    arms unfurled to heaven in the sun.
A woman in gray strapless steers between this net
        of tables and the church, her blonde bun
slipping loose. Shaded by canvas and sheaves
    of artificial palm, I sense
evening coming on, as Thomas surely did,
        your favorite saint, who had
    to touch the wound of light to believe.

I order a parfait. Around me, couples talk,
sipping summer wine with beaded bubbles—
    someone laughs and says, *Tak, tak*—
and the waitress weaves between tables
        carrying my dish, tall as a vase,
and a long-handled spoon. The first bite's
    crisp as a chilled corsage,
fragrant then tart. I pretend the second bite
        is yours. Would you taste
    frozen roses? Or some perfumed mirage?

    I go on eating, pretending. Is this
what widows do? Imagining a kiss,
    conversing with the air, while all around
real lovers, fingers interlaced,
        dream of solitude? Even in June
I dread the coming sleet and wind,

so harsh on your lungs. But today,
licking the cold petals from this spoon,
       I can almost feel, a continent away,
the flutter of your impatient hands.

At Daily Mass on the Feast of the Holy Innocents

Rachael Graham

My sorrow swells within my breasts again.
They hear before my ears the infant's cry
and surge with milk that feeds no one but pain.
God, my eyes did not take this long to dry.

To hide the two wet circles on my shirt,
I force my scarf to flow around my chest.
Across the room, another woman shifts
her clothes and bares a tender swollen breast.

Her baby's cries are stifled on her teat,
and mine are silenced by propriety.
But you, seeing me swallow our son's name,
you kiss my hand and curse my piety.

Memorial Sloan-Kettering

Judith Valente

David's mother wheels him across the deck
    outside of pediatrics
        St. Patrick's Day morning.
            He wants to feel the sun on his neck.

Purple crocuses
    in red flower boxes lift their tongues to the sun,
        a chill wind crosses the parapet.
            David sends his mother inside for a blanket.

Jesus will pull him through
    David's mother tells the Moslem chaplain.
        She doesn't care what God he prays to:
            Allah, Jehovah, Bahá'u'lláh.

People take what comfort they can find
    the imam says.
        He once heard a man in Room 309 confide
            Leukemia saved my life.

For 20 years the imam has washed and shrouded
    bodies at Malcolm Shabazz,
        swears he's seen smiles
            on the faces of the dead.

David draws his blanket
    across white slipper socks, striped flannel robe.
        Dilaudid flows from his broviac line
            in a thin rivulet.

Who will inscribe his name in the book of life?

Pietà

Paul Mariani

New Year's Eve, a party at my brother's.
Hats, favors, the whole shebang, as we waited
for one world to die into another.

And still it took three martinis before
she could bring herself to say it. How
the body of her grown son lay alone there

in the ward, just skin & bone, the nurses
masked & huddled in the doorway, afraid
to cross over into a world no one seemed

to understand. This was a dozen years ago,
you have to understand, before the thing
her boy had became a household word.

Consider Martha. Consider Lazarus four days gone.
If only you'd been here, she says, if only
you'd been here. And no one now to comfort her,

no one except this priest, she says, an old
friend who'd stood beside them through the dark
night of it all, a bull-like man, skin black

as the black he wore, the only one who seemed
willing to walk across death's threshold into
that room. And now, she says, when the death

was over, to see him lift her son, light as a baby
with the changes death had wrought, and cradle him
like that, then sing him on his way, a cross

between a lullaby & blues, *mmm hmmm*, while
the nurses, still not understanding what they saw,
stayed outside and watched them from the door.

Elegy for the Saint
of Letting Small Fish Go

Eliot Khalil Wilson

I.

You too might step into a puddle of fire,
or splash through a stream of glowing lava
where only moments before you were barefoot
in your kitchen after a late night of too much wine
and, nearly naked, frying bacon at the stove.

A burn like this is a different thing the doctor said
and I can believe it. I was a different thing.

I was a man with an unquenchable oil well fire on his feet
that would blaze up as the medicine ebbed.
And the skin curled over, brown-red,
too much like the meat I was cooking in the pan that I dropped
—an irony not lost on even the youngest of nurses
drinking and bacon don't mix
she kidded as I healed.

Yet had my wounds burned like Vulcan's forge
they'd be a distant fire in light of the child
behind the glass in the opposite bed.

II.

Where were you saints when the fire first licked his hands?
Hadn't he in living prayed to you?

I want the saint of ice cream trucks
to turn off the carnival, climb down, and explain it all—
        account for all the betrayers—
The saints of reachable branches and bank envelope lollipops,
the saints of his mother's cool arms, of new basketball shoes, and

professional wrestling.
The saints of tree forts, pocket knives, and stadium food.
The saints of waffles and eyebrows and box turtles.
The saint of jam.
The saint of his own bed.
Where were you saints of wheelies and rodeo clowns and rockets?

III.
I was at home when the sepsis took him
and they wheeled him to that all-light room
and when they covered his face.

Yet I had seen his grafts and debridements,
the twice daily baths and dressings,
and the shock at that last turn of gauze
—how the fire bit at his summer legs and arms—
black skin, blacker still, and red.

I was there to see the lost mother
who would live in fire for the child she had known.
There to see all who entered shake their heads
as if wondering as I wondered
how so small a thing can carry such pain
—pain that pushed through the morphine push—
—pain that conquered even those numbing Nordic gods—
Vicodin, Ativan, and Tylox.

It is not my place.
He was not my child,
and I could never speak to him,
but hold him out of the fire.
I would not have him burned again.

Give him back to rocking water,
to pendulum down through the fingers of the sun.
Let the ocean run his veins and heart—
     full, then empty, then full again.

Or return him to the folding ground,
face up to the sky.
A boon for dreamlessness,
this petty thief of time.

Then Sings My Soul

Paul Mariani

Who can tell a man's real pain
when he learns the news at last
that he must die? Sure we all know
none of us is going anywhere
except in some pine-slab box or its fine
expensive equal. But don't we put it off
another day, and then another and another,
as I suppose we must to cope? And so
with Lenny, Leonardo Rodriquez, a man
in the old world mold, a Spaniard
of great dignity and fine humility,
telling us on this last retreat for men
that he had finally given up praying
because he didn't want to hear
what God might want to tell him now:
that he wanted Lenny, soon, in spite
of the hard facts that he had his kids,
his still beautiful wife, and an aged
mother to support. I can tell you now
it hit us hard, him telling us, because
for me as for the others he'd been
the model, had been a leader, raised
in the old faith of San Juan de la Cruz
and Santa Teresa de Avila, this toreador
waving the red flag at death itself,
horns lowered and hurling down on him.
This story has no ending because there is
still life and life means hope. But
on the third day, at the last Mass, we were
all sitting in one big circle like something
out of Dante—fifty laymen, a priest, a nun—

with Guido DiPietro playing his guitar
and singing an old hymn in that tenor voice
of his, all of us joining in at the refrain,
Then sings my soul, my Savior God to thee,
How great thou art, how great thou art,
and there I was on Lenny's left, listening
to him sing, his voice cracked with resignation,
how great thou art, until angry glad tears
began rolling down my face, surprising me. . . .
Lord, listen to the sound of my voice.
Grant Lenny health and long life. Or,
if not that, whatever strength and peace
he needs. His family likewise, and
his friends. Grant me too the courage
to face death when it shall notice me,
when I shall still not understand why
there is so much sorrow in the world.
Teach me to stare down those lowered horns
on the dead-end street that shall have no alleys
and no open doors. And grant me the courage
then to still sing to thee, *how great thou art*.

Into the Night

J. D. Schraffenberger

Old man Joe believed that life should be
cut off in the sound and living part,
according to the surgeon's rule in amputations,
and if he could be neither sound nor living,
in the truest sense, he was, then, already
too late and should forthwith pack it in—
thus his desperate seizing on that second lucky
life, no longer lived in takes but in the long
lovely moment. *You're listening to . . . Music . . .*
Into the Night . . . But O ho ho . . . *I'm your host . . .*
Those in the know know . . . *Joseph Johnstone . . .*
Behold the old-man spittle on the microphone . . .
That of course . . . was J. S. Bach's . . . Saint Matthew Passion . . .
the beastly hook of his nose . . . *Coming up next . . .*

Who Dies of Thirst

Mary Jane Nealon

On my desk the dahlia is a fisted door,
is a feather falling between myself and the man I am trying to
    help:
train-jumper, *transient*. After three days in the Thompson Falls jail
his body's rancid scent overwhelms me. He is a criminal trespasser.

I go with an escort to his trailer, which straddles a ravine.
The rusted shell explodes with mice, attracts
a red-winged hawk. The sky is a berth behind the circling
hawk, I escape for a moment in the wing's spiked tip.
We leave medicines, lift the wire fence back in place.

I latch the day. Across the road a spitting llama
rolls in pink flowers. Inside, in my gut, a cramp
of what I no longer want to give away.
I am tired of serving people.

=

I believed I would live like Kateri Tekawitha.
Disfigured, she leaned over the parched lips of Indians,
caught in their blistering smallpox.

I would rise everyday into goodness, place
cool cloths on foreheads, make pumices
and plasters, and then at death,
like hers, my scars would rapturously fade.

I would ascend, luminescent.
This was the wildflower story I was living in.

But my back gave out from lifting bodies in their beds,
from leaning over the colostomy's rosy stoma.

I resented the way people held on to me, in labor,
in death. I saw birth as a *tearing away* of flesh.

I carried my imagined *real* life in a metal cart strapped
to my ankles. Everywhere I looked: faces,
when all I wanted was the empty desert.

Red rock of the free life.
Carved wall of the vacant cave.
I ate delicious words when I was alone.
What will I be if I am not a caretaker? My hands
are flat expressions of themselves, are unrecognizable.

=

This morning, an explosion of gnats and flies,
sweet maple window
drawing them to *this* life, as I am drawn to leave mine.
I call in sick
and fall into Salmon Lake
which has become a kind of room where green
is nothing more than a cool cool day.
Lake, open and rocky, my hands are returned to me
as they pass over lily pads and shift the silt
that coats dark water. The floating leaves are words,
words are bubbles that rise to the surface
circling my thighs. Words smell like pine.

=

The lake is a velvet confessional,
I kneel in its arms. The lake is thought, and memory.
In the water, my dead brother rises clean of agony,
and we are watching art slides after school
with my father. Our knees touch in the dark
as we practice dry, innocent kisses on our hands.
The lake is the gold parlor of my childhood.

The lake is a book. The lake is my first lover,
my best lover. The lake is the moon we thought we would
   colonize.
The lake is the colony we named Lorca.

In the distance a siren heads down Highway 83,
and the sound of a child falling sounds like a child
falling away. The day moves from east to west over water.

Can I be left in my cool lake?
Can I *be* the cool lake?

Limbo: Altered States

Mary Karr

No sooner does the plane angle up
than I cork off to dream a bomb blast:
A fireball roiling through the cabin in slo-mo,
seat blown loose from its bolts,
I hang weightless a nanosecond
      in blue space

then jerk awake to ordered rows.
And there's the silver liquor cart jangling
its thousand bells, the perfect doses
of juniper gin and oak-flavored scotch
      held by a rose-nailed hand.

I don't miss drinking, don't miss
driving into shit with more molecular density
than myself, nor the *Mission Impossible*
reruns I sat before, nor the dead
space inside only alcohol could fill and then
      not even. But I miss

the aftermath, the pure simplicity:
mouth parched, head hissing static.
How little I asked of myself then—to suck
the next breath, suffer the next heave, live
till cocktail hour when I could mix
      the next sickness.

I locked the bathroom door, sat
on the closed commode, shirtless,
in filmy underpants telling myself that death
could fit my grasp and be staved off
while in the smeary shaving glass,

I practiced the stillness of a soul
      awaiting birth.

For the *real* that swarmed beyond the door
I was pure scorn, dead center of my stone and starless
universe, orbited by no one. Novitiate obliterate, Saint
Absence, Duchess of Naught . . .
A stinging ether folded me in mist.

Sometimes landing the head's pressure's enormous.
When my plane tilts down, houses grow large, streets
lose their clear geometry. The leafy earth soon fills my portal,
and in the gray graveyard of cars, a stick figure
becomes my son in royal blue cap flapping his arms
as if to rise. Thank god for our place
in this forest of forms, for the *gravitas*
that draws me back to him, and for how lightly
      lightly I touch down.

Being Called Back

Kelli Russell Agodon

Nevertheless its steps can be heard . . .
—Pablo Neruda, *"Nothing But Death"*

In case of accident, call a priest,
      or so reads the back of
my Saint Christopher medallion.

And I want to engrave:
      Or 911. Or an ambulance,
but not just the priest.

I know the priest would come,
      offer everlasting life and pray
over my body, but I'm betting

on the medic, the EMT, the blonde girl
      who works weekends at the fire station
to keep her daughter in private school.

I put my faith in the hands of these saviors
      before I'll kiss the white collar
of the man who loves God the same way I love life.

I'm not ready to be called back. Not now.
      Maybe when my body begins to crumble
and needs every speck of energy to leave

a chair or revise a poem, then I will say:
      Just the priest please.
But for now, call anyone

you think could help, anyone
        who could pull me from the land of afterlife
where "eternal bliss" *sounds* lovely,

roaming the clouds with dead relatives
        or wandering a white fog
near the wings of a friend who died too young.

I imagine yards of cotton unrolling.
        God is remodeling the space
for the eighty million new souls

who will visit this year, souls climbing
        the new spiral staircase.
It will be enchanting to encounter people

who have passed before me. I'll make a point
        to ask Neruda about death
dressed as a broom, as I keep believing I'll be swept up.

The Usual

Sandra Duguid

*Those who have not experienced the glow engendered on one's
entering the coffeeshop, and having the server inquire, "the Usual?"
are poor indeed.*

*For who wants to stay home? We know, for good or ill, that
we belong there; the comfort of domesticity may be great, indeed,
but it is not convivial.*

*No, the Idle-Hour, Coffee-Corner, Coffee-Cup, where even the
stranger may still find himself addressed as "Hon"—that is the place
for me.*

—David Mamet

One always knows what to expect
in a diner—
with a name like Fireside,
The Rainbow, or Chester—
broad muffins shining in clear wrap
by the counter juke box
checked with all the letters
of the alphabet
and numbers—1–0;
ketsup, a sugar dispenser—
silver, its top flap;
a black cubed,
open-mouthed
napkin holder.

The decor will never
betray you—
look for a fake
brick wall; coach lamps
outside restrooms,

out-of-scale chandeliers,
spider plants,
a mighty shouldered beverage dispenser,
half cantalopes
peaked,
look for the orbiting cakes.

Always, at the salad bar
flaking chunks
of feta cheese,
and something—like tapioca—
wrapped in leaves;
a swirl of orange
curls in the neighboring dressing;
lettuce, tomatoes, onions shine
colorful as Christmas.

On your placemat, fantasies—
for Custom T-shirt Printing,
Prestige Volvo, affordable
auto insurance for Jersey drivers,
silk screening at The Harbor,
Singing Strings School in Livingston—
the Suzuki approach
to violin, viola, violin-cello.

Not that rumors of life gone wrong
don't leak in—
newspapers at the door
rack up
local and foreign murders;
a diagram on the wall
instructs us, step by step
in the Heimlich.

Nonetheless, one sometimes wishes,
for all the Bible's

splendid descriptions,
for all the Saints' visions,
paradise could be like this—
something instantly recognizable
by eye or hand—
graspable
as a carmel or brown
coffee decanter,
or a silver-mounded salt
or pepper shaker
on a booth
or a full, round table,
where, when you walk in
through Windexed glass doors,
and are seated
hungry, expectant,
the waitress, alert,
note pad ready,
pencil carried
at some familiar angle
extending through space and time
sings out
in four clear tones,
"What can I get you, Hon?"

St. Peter's B-list

Jake Oresick

I sometimes think
About the nightlife in heaven,
And I wonder if there isn't
A dark spot on the East Side
Where on weekends Eva Cassidy sings
To dimly-lit tables in the clouds.

Churchill sits
With Thom Jefferson and Sally,
Guzzling scotch and, for once,
Saying nothing.

King David hustles pool
And struts about in a Speedo,
He nods to Michelangelo,
Who is, again,
With his close friend Gary.

Jack and Bobby are fused
To their bar stools, and run
Lines by Jessica Simpson,
Who, I know, isn't dead,
But so what? And she giggles
And beams and wonders
Just who they are.

When it's my time to go,
I think I'll find some dark dive—
Dollar drafts, not too loud.
I'd like to sit with
Has-been sitcom stars,
Constantine's Harem,

Guys who played
Minor league baseball.
I'd like to hear history
Told from the street,
From the boy staring hungrily
Through the butcher's window.

Afterword

The lives of the saints are poems.

In other words, one cannot fully understand a saint's life from a purely rationalistic point of view. Strictly speaking, they do not make "sense."

It makes no earthly "sense" for St. Damien of Molokai to move to the Island of Molokai, work with those who have contracted leprosy, contract the disease himself, and then die. The earthly mind says: "That doesn't make sense; he could have done more for people if he avoided the illness, and lived a longer life." It makes little sense for Mother Teresa to leave her original religious order, found a brand-new order for women in the slums of Calcutta, and care for the poor in simple hospices, affording them dignity in death. The modern mind says: "That's absurd; she would have done better by putting them in a hospital with the latest technology, where they would have gotten better medical care instead of kind words from a few nuns." It makes no sense for St. Francis of Assisi to respond to a mysterious dream in which God asks him to rebuild the Church. The post-Freudian mind says, "That's foolish. It's only a dream."

But the lives of the saints cannot be understood unless seen as works of art, as poems. They can only be understood as songs of praise to God.

Emily Dickinson wrote, "If I feel physically as if the top of my head were taken off, I know that is poetry." The saints' lives should make us feel the same. When you read about a saint, or if you are lucky enough to meet one or watch him or her in action, you should be disoriented. The saints' lives shock, and they should.

Something similar is at work in Jesus' parables. When asked about the reign of God, Jesus does not respond with a tightly wound theological definition, but with an open-ended story or a poetic image. Jesus tells his listeners about a mustard seed, or a woman sweeping her house, or a man finding a treasure. He offered poetic means to help people grasp a concept impossible to understand otherwise.

And when asked, "Who is my neighbor?" Jesus does not answer with the five essential elements that define a neighbor; he instead tells them a story about a man who was attacked by robbers as he made his way from Jerusalem to Jericho. These poetic tales must have made people in Jesus' day feel that the tops of their heads were being taken off. Some people responded to the shock and disorientation by living in a new way; others responded by plotting Jesus' death.

The great scripture scholar C. H. Dodd said that a parable is "a metaphor or simile drawn from nature or common life, arresting the hearer by its vividness or strangeness, and leaving the mind in sufficient doubt about its precise application to tease it into active thought." Note the similarity to the poem, with its metaphors and similes, which is similarly designed to "tease" the mind.

The most important truths about God are not reached with definitions and proofs but by poems and stories. And by people: the saints. That is why this book is a treasure. These poets take the lives of the saints as they are meant to be understood: as poems. From human works of art they draw out literary ones.

You are called to be a saint, too. What will your poem be?

James Martin, S.J.

Acknowledgments

"Absolution" is from *Immaculate Fuel* by Mary Jane Nealon. Copyright 2004 by Mary Jane Nealon. Reprinted by permission of the Permissions Company, Inc., on behalf of Four Way Books, www.fourwaybooks.com.

"After Saying *The Chaplet of the Divine Mercy*" by Karen Kovacik is used by permission of the author. All rights reserved.

"Agápe" by Timothy Murphy is from *Mortal Stakes/Faint Thunder* (The Dakota Institute Press, 2011). Copyright 2011 by The Dakota Institute Press. Reprinted by permission of the author.

"All Hallow's Eve" by Joseph Bathanti is from *This Metal* (Press 53, 2011). Copyright 2011 by Joseph Bathanti. Reprinted by permission of the author.

"All Saints Day" by Kevin Brown is used by permission of the author. All rights reserved.

"The American Cathedral" by Alan Berecka is from *Remembering the Body* (Mongrel Empire Press, 2011). Copyright 2011 by Alan Berecka. Reprinted by permission of the author.

"The Angel with the Broken Wing" is from *Pity the Beautiful* by Dana Gioia. Copyright 2012 by Dana Gioia. Reprinted by permission of Graywolf Press.

"Anonymity" by Meredith Kunsa is reprinted by permission of the author. First published in *The Raven Chronicles*.

"Another Mary" by Laurie Byro is used by permission of the author. All rights reserved.

"Apocalypse Island" by Nicholas Samaras is used by permission of the author. All rights reserved.

"Desert Ascent, John of Climachus" by Trina Gaynon is used by permission of the author. All rights reserved.

"Double Saints Day" by Helen Ruggieri is used by permission of the author. All rights reserved.

"Elegy for a Living Man" by Dean Kostos is from *Celestial Rust* (Red Dust, Inc., 1994). Copyright 1994 by Dean Kostos. Reprinted by permission of the author.

"Elegy for the Saint of Letting Small Fish Go" by Eliot Khalil Wilson is from *The Saint of Letting Small Fish Go* (Cleveland State University Poetry Center, 2003). Copyright 2003 by Eliot Khalil Wilson. Reprinted by permission of the author.

"Faith" by Maria Terrone is reprinted by permission of the author. First published in *Crab Orchard Review*.

"The Fannie Situation" by Jamison Lee is used by permission of the author. All rights reserved.

"Fathom" is from *Inventory at the All-Night Drugstore* by Erika Meitner. Copyright 2003 by Erika Meitner. Reprinted by permission of Anhinga Press.

"The Feast of St. Anthony" by Gerry LaFemina is used by permission of the author. All rights reserved.

"The Feast of Stephen" by Joseph Bathanti is from *Anson County* (Press 53, 2013). Copyright 2013 by Joseph Bathanti. Reprinted by permission of the author.

"Girl Saints" by CX Dillhunt is from *Girl Saints* (Fireweed Press, 2003). Copyright 2003 by CX Dillhunt. Reprinted by permission of the author.

"Limbo: Altered States" by Mary Karr is from *Viper Rum* (Penguin, 1994). Copyright 1994 by Mary Karr. Reprinted by permission of the author.

"The Lives of the Saints" is from *The Lives of the Saints* by Suzanne Paola. Copyright 2002 by Suzanne Paola. Reprinted by permission of University of Washington Press.

"The Maculardegeneration Boogie" by Jim Daniels is used by permission of the author. All rights reserved.

"The Mad Nun" is from *Daily Horoscope* by Dana Gioia. Copyright 1986 by Dana Gioia. Reprinted by permission of Graywolf Press.

"Manhattan" by Paul Mariani is from *The Great Wheel* (W. W. Norton & Co., 1996). Copyright 1996 by Paul Mariani. Reprinted by permission of the author.

"Memorial Sloan-Kettering" by Judith Valente is from *Discovering Moons* (Virtual Artists Collective, 2009). Copyright 2009 by Judith Valente. Reprinted by permission of the author.

"Miracle Blanket" is from *Ideal Cities* by Erika Meitner. Copyright 2010 by Erika Meitner. Reprinted by permission of HarperCollins Publishers, Inc.

Excerpt from *Niagara Falls* is from *Niagara Falls* by Jim Daniels. Copyright 1994 by Jim Daniels. Reprinted by permission of Adastra Press.

"Nicaraguan Morning Grounds" by Rebecca Lauren is used by permission of the author. All rights reserved.

"Ode to Saint Barbara of the Barbara Shoppe" by Rebecca Lauren is used by permission of the author. All rights reserved.

"Offering to Saint Roch" by Melinda Palacio is reprinted by permission of the author. First published in *The Más Tequila Review*.

"Portrait of Myself at Fourteen, as Saint Rose of Lima" is from *In the Human Zoo* by Jennifer Perrine. Copyright 2011 by Jennifer Perrine. Reprinted by permission of University of Utah Press.

"Praying to St. Stephen's Hand" by Susanna Rich is reprinted by permission of the author. First published at www.literarybohemian.com.

"The Priesthood" is from *Immaculate Fuel* by Mary Jane Nealon. Copyright 2004 by Mary Jane Nealon. Reprinted by permission of The Permissions Company, Inc., on behalf of Four Way Books, www.fourwaybooks.com.

"Proximity" is from *The Second Person* by C. Dale Young. Copyright 2007 by C. Dale Young. Reprinted by permission of The Permissions Company, Inc., on behalf of Four Way Books, www.fourwaybooks.com.

"Rome, *Santa Marie en Cosmedin*, 11/14" by Wendy Vardaman is reprinted by permission of the author. First published at www.expressmilwaukee.com.

"Rose-Flavored Ice Cream with Tart Cherries" by Karen Kovacik is used by permission of the author. All rights reserved.

"Saint Anthony's Day" by Charlotte Barr is from *The Text Beneath* (Parson's Porch Books, 2010). Copyright 2010 by Charlotte Barr. Reprinted by permission of the author.

"Saint Francis at Yoga" by Susan Blackwell Ramsey is used by permission of the author. All rights reserved.

"Sainthood" by Joseph Bathanti is from *Restoring Sacred Art* (Star Cloud Press, 2010). Copyright 2010 by Joseph Bathanti. Reprinted by permission of the author.

"Saint Joe Considers the Furnace" is from *Saint Joe's Passion* by J. D. Schraffenberger. Copyright 2008 by J. D. Schraffenberger. Reprinted

"Shopping for Miracles: Lourdes, 1979" by Alan Berecka is from *Remembering the Body* (Mongrel Empire Press, 2011). Copyright 2011 by Alan Berecka. Reprinted by permission of the author.

"Song for Saint Nicholas Day" by Terry Kirts is from *To the Refrigerator Gods* (Seven Kitchens Press, 2010). Copyright 2010 by Terry Kirts. Reprinted by permission of the author.

"*Sotto Voce*" is from *The Second Person* by C. Dale Young. Copyright 2007 by C. Dale Young. Reprinted by permission of The Permissions Company, Inc., on behalf of Four Way Books, www.fourwaybooks.com.

"The Special Guest" is from *Return to the City of White Donkeys* by James Tate. Copyright 2004 by James Tate. Reprinted by permission of HarperCollins Publishers, Inc.

"Spiritual Exercises in a Cellar Bookstore" by Brett Foster is from *Fall Run Road* (Finishing Line Press, 2012). Copyright 2012 by Brett Foster. Reprinted by permission of the author.

"Spokes" by Kristina Roth is used by permission of the author. All rights reserved.

"St. Agnes, Pink-Slipped" by Ann Cefola is from *St. Agnes, Pink-Slipped* (Kattywompus Press, 2011). Copyright 2011 by Ann Cefola. Reprinted by permission of the author.

"The Story I Like Best about Saint Teresa—" by Susan Blackwell Ramsey is reprinted by permission of the author. First published in *Folio*.

"St. Pachomius of the Unemployed" by Alessandra Simmons is used by permission of the author. All rights reserved.

"St. Peter, 1957" is from *Dragonfly Dance* by Denise K. Lajimodiere. Copyright 2010 by Denise K. Lajimodiere. Reprinted by permission of Michigan State University Press.

"Waiting for Ecstasy" is from *Moving House* by Angela Alaimo O'Donnell. Copyright 2009 by Angela Alaimo O'Donnell. Reprinted by permission of WordTech Communications.

"Watching You, Mother, Almost Thanksgiving, St. Jude's I.C.U." by Susanna Rich is used by permission of the author. All rights reserved.

"What Physics Teaches Us" is from *A Garment Sewn from Night Itself* by Gerry LaFemina. Copyright 2003 by Gerry LaFemina. Reprinted by permission of the author.

"When, at Last, I Meet My Mother Again" is from *In the Human Zoo* by Jennifer Perrine. Copyright 2011 by Jennifer Perrine. Reprinted by permission of University of Utah Press.

"Who Dies of Thirst" is from *Immaculate Fuel* by Mary Jane Nealon. Copyright 2004 by Mary Jane Nealon. Reprinted by permission of The Permissions Company, Inc., on behalf of Four Way Books, www.four waybooks.com.

Appendix I: The Saints

Agnes. Feast day January 21; virgin, martyr; b. Rome, ca. 292; d. Rome, ca. 305. She was martyred during the persecution of Diocletian in the Stadium Domitian on the site of the present day Piazza Navona. She was said to be very beautiful and denied many suitors for her hand because she had dedicated her maidenhood to God. In one legend, she was sent to a brothel as punishment, and one man went blind when he looked at her lustfully. She prayed for his cure and then was sent on to her martyrdom. She is the patron saint of young girls.

Aloysius Gonzaga. Feast day June 21; b. Castiglione, near Mantua, Italy, March 9, 1568; d. Rome, June 21, 1591. His charity was revealed in the catechetical lessons he gave and in his care for the sick. While attending the sick during an epidemic in Rome in March 1591, he contracted the plague and died three months later. He is the patron saint of young people and students of Jesuit colleges and universities.

Anthony of Padua. Feast day June 13; Franciscan Doctor of the Church; b. Lisbon, Portugal, (August 15), 1195; d. Arcella, near Padua, Italy, June 13, 1231. In 1223, Francis of Assisi appointed Anthony the first professor of theology for the friars; he is credited with introducing the theology of St. Augustine to the Franciscan Order. Commonly prayed to as the finder of lost objects, he is the patron of lovers, marriage, pregnant women, and miners.

Apollonia of Alexandria. Feast day February 9; virgin, martyr; birth date and origin unknown; d. Alexandria, Egypt, 248. An aged deaconess of Alexandria, she was martyred during an anti-Christian riot. As she was attacked, her teeth were knocked out by numerous blows to her face. She was then taken to a bonfire and told to renounce her faith or be fed to the flames, at which point she walked into the fire. She is the patron saint of dentists and those suffering from toothaches.

Augustine. Feast day August 28; bishop, philosopher, theologian, Doctor of the Church; b. Thagaste in Numidia, North Africa, November 13, 354; d. Hippo, August 28, 430. After a spiritual crisis, he converted to Christianity in 387. He went on to become one of the most influential figures of the early Church, especially in defending Church orthodoxy against such schisms as Manichaeism, Donatism, and Pelagianism. St. Jerome called him "the second founder of the faith." He is the patron saint of theologians.

Barbara. Feast day December 4; virgin, martyr; dates and origin unknown (200–350?). She is the subject of a popular romance in Caxton's version of *The Golden Legend*, but there is little evidence of an actual historical figure. In the legend, her father, nervous of her beauty and an array of suitors, placed Barbara in a tower. Upon her release, the father learned that Barbara had become a Christian and would not marry. Eventually, he had her executed. At the moment of her death, a lightning bolt reduced the father to ash. She is the patron saint of those in peril by lightning, firefighters, artillerymen, stonemasons, architects, and builders.

Bartholomew. Feast day August 24; apostle, martyr; dates unknown (first century). He is mentioned as one of the twelve apostles in Matthew, Mark, Luke, and Acts, but he is replaced by a Nathanael in the Gospel of John. Tradition has it that he was a missionary in India, Phrygia, Lycaonia, Mesopotamia, and Persia. He is thought to have been martyred by being flayed alive in Armenia. He is the patron saint of Armenia and tanners.

Benedict. Feast day July 11; monastic founder; b. Nursia, Italy, ca. 480; d. Monte Cassino, Italy, ca. 547. He is the author of an influential monastic rule; the Benedictine Order is named for him. Ironically, Benedict barely survived his first assignment as abbot when his charges tried to poison him. Tradition has it that the cup containing the poisoned wine broke when blessed by Benedict. He is the patron saint of kidney disease and students.

Bernadette of Lourdes. Feast day April 16; virgin, mystic; b. Lourdes, southwestern France, January 7, 1844; d. Nevers, France, April 16, 1879. The daughter of an impoverished miller, Bernadette had eighteen visions of the Blessed Virgin Mary between February 11 and July 16, 1858. After the apparitions, Bernadette was educated by the Sisters of Charity and Christian Instruction of Nevers. In 1866, she joined the congregation at the motherhouse in Nevers. She is the patroness of shepherds and shepherdesses and people ridiculed for their faith.

Bonaventure. Feast day July 15; Franciscan saint, scholar, seventh general minister of the Lesser Brothers (*friars minor*), cardinal bishop of Albano, Doctor of the Church; b. Bagnoregio, Italy, 1217; d. Lyons, France, July 15, 1274. He stands in contrast to his contemporary St. Thomas Aquinas. Bonaventure favored a more affective than reasoned approach to God, arguing that a fool's love may have greater knowledge of God than a humanly wise man. He is the patron saint of workers.

Bridget of Sweden. Feast day July 23; foundress of the Bridgettines; b. Upland, principal province of Sweden, 1302 or 1303; d. Rome, 1373. She married young and had eight children. Her daughter Catherine (of Vadstena) also became a saint. At one point, she was appointed lady-in-waiting to the Queen of Sweden. After the death of her husband, Bridget became a nun and founded a dual monastery/convent at Vadstena. She spent her last years in Rome and going on pilgrimages. She is the patron saint of nuns and Sweden.

Catherine of Alexandria. Feast day November 25; martyr; birth date unknown; d. Alexandria, Egypt, date unknown (fourth century?). Little if any evidence supports the actual existence of the saint. According to tradition, she was born of an aristocratic family in Alexandria and later converted to Christianity. At some point, an emperor tried to get her to renounce her faith by various means, but she out-argued fifty pagan philosophers and turned down the chance to be the emperor's courtesan. She was imprisoned, where she was visited by visions of Christ, fed by a dove, and tortured on a wheel, but the wheel flew apart and killed some soldiers. She was finally beheaded. She is the patron saint of philosophers, young women, preachers, nurses, and craftsmen.

Catherine of Siena. Feast day April 29; Dominican tertiary, mystic, Doctor of the Church, reformer of popes; b. Siena, ca. 1347; d. Rome, April 29, 1380. Catherine ranks high among Catholic mystics and spiritual writers. Her teachings are centered on the creative and redemptive nature of God's love. She is a patron saint of Europe, Italy, and nursing.

Christopher. Feast day July 25; dates unknown. According to tradition, he was a Canaanite of great strength and stature who carried the Christ Child across a river on his shoulders. In the Middle Ages, a popular belief existed that looking at an image of the saint would keep one from harm for one day. This belief led to the installation of his picture in many churches. He is the patron saint of travelers, sailors, and motorists. In 1969, due to a lack of historical evidence, his feast day was removed from the universal calendars, but it may still be observed.

Clare of Assisi. Feast day August 11; foundress of the Order of Poor Clares; b. Assisi, Italy, 1193 or 1194; d. Monastery of San Damiano outside the walls of Assisi, August 11, 1253. Like Francis, she was a member of an aristocratic family of Assisi. Upon hearing Francis preach, she too dedicated her life to poverty and service. She founded the Order of the Poor Clares. She is the patron saint of embroiderers, good weather, those in childbirth, and sufferers of eye disease. In 1958, she was named the patron saint of television.

Colman of Kilmacduagh. Feast day October 29; hermit, bishop; b. Corker in Kilatran, Ireland, dates unknown (mid-sixth century); d. Ireland, ca. 632. Reportedly, he sought solitude in Burren in the mountains of County Clare because he had been made a bishop against his will. Along with one disciple, he subsisted on a diet of wild vegetables and water. He founded a monastery at Kilmacduagh. The land for the monastery was given to him by a king who was transported to Colman's cell by angels.

Cosmas and Damian. Feast day September 27; martyrs; b. date and place unknown; d. Cyr, Syria, late fifth century. Twin brothers who practiced medicine without charging a fee, they were martyred together for their faith. Many churches were dedicated to them, and the faithful often slept in the churches in hopes of being cured. They are the patron saints of physicians.

Dominic Savio. Feast day March 9; b. San Giovanni, Italy, April 2, 1842; d. Mondonio, Italy, March 9, 1857. Described as a spiritually precocious student of St. John Bosco, he died young of tuberculosis. He is the patron saint of choirboys and youths in general.

Dominic. Feast day August 8; founder of the Order of Preachers, or Dominicans; b. Caleruega, Castile (Spain), ca. 1170; d. Bologna, Italy, August 6, 1221. Devoted to spreading the faith through appeals to hearts and minds, Dominic conceived an order of highly trained priests who would teach and preach far and wide. As a young priest, he once sold his books and furniture to raise money for the poor in a time of famine. Priests in his order take a vow of poverty. He is the patron saint of scientists, astronomers, and the Dominican Republic.

Dorothy Day. Social activist, author, lecturer; b. Bath Beach, Brooklyn, November 8, 1897; d. November 27, 1980. At present, her "cause for canonization" is open, meriting her the title of "Servant of God." She converted to Catholicism in 1928, shortly after the birth of her daughter. In the 1930s, she was influenced by the teaching of Peter Maurin and set about trying to solve the three main problems of the age: war, poverty, and depersonalization. She went on to found *The Catholic Worker* newspaper and houses for the poor in more than forty cities. She was an ardent pacifist who rejected the notion of a just war.

Dymphna. Feast day May 15; virgin, martyr; dates and origin unknown. Her body was found in the thirteenth century; the name Dymphna was on a brick on her coffin. Legend has it she was the Christian daughter of a pagan prince. When her mother died, the father sought out Dymphna, who had been living as a solitary, and tried to seduce her. When she refused his advances, he killed her. Her bones were said to be able to restore the insane. This led to a large asylum being built in Gheel, a Flemish town near Antwerp. She is the patron saint of the mentally ill.

Edith Stein (Teresa Benedicta of the Cross). Feast day August 9; martyr, Carmelite nun, philosopher; b. Wrocław (Breslau in Prussian Silesia), Poland, October 12, 1891; d. Birkenau section of Auschwitz concentration camp, August 9, 1942. Born of devout Jewish parents, she became a student of Edmund Husserl, the founder of phenomenology. She converted and was baptized on January 1, 1922. Upon her canonization, Pope John Paul II named her a copatron of Europe. He also encouraged the reading of her works, which include *The Science of the Cross* and *Finite and Eternal Being*.

Faustina (Maria Faustina Kowalska). Feast day October 5; mystic, nun of the Congregation of the Blessed Virgin Mary of Mercy; b. Glogowiec, Poland, August 25, 1905; d. Kraków, Poland, October 5, 1938. In 2002, she became the first Polish female saint canonized by Pope John Paul II. A cloistered nun who was assigned to menial tasks, she had numerous visions of Jesus and Mary, which she wrote about in her diary, *Divine Mercy in My Soul.* Originally banned by the Vatican, a better translation of her diary was commissioned by Cardinal Karol Wojtyła six months before he became pope.

The Forty Martyrs of Sebaste. Feast day March 10; soldiers, martyrs; d. Sabastea, Turkey, 320. During the persecution of Emperor Licinius, Christians were given the choice of renouncing their faith or being put to death. In Sebastea, forty members of the famed Thundering Legion appeared before the local tribunal and proclaimed their faith. After several attempts to have them renounce the faith, the local governor devised a plan in which the men were stripped naked and told to stand on a frozen lake. On the banks of the lake, fires were lit and hot baths were drawn to induce the men, but only one man left the group and was replaced by another soldier who had been converted. The men died of exposure.

Francis of Assisi. Feast day October 4; founder of the Franciscan Order and the Order of Poor Clares; b. Assisi, Italy, ca. 1182; d. Assisi, October 3, 1226. Often referred to as the "greatest saint," he renounced a life of wealth to live in poverty, simplicity, and humility. This conversion was in part a response to a crucifix in San Damiano that asked Francis to rebuild his house. Two years before the saint's death, he received the first recorded stigmata. Francis is the patron saint of Italy, Catholic Action, animals, zoos, and the environment.

George. Feast day April 23; martyr; dates unknown (third or fourth century). He most likely died in Lydda (present-day Lod in Israel) during the persecution of Diocletian and Maximian. Stories about him were popularized in the book *The Golden Legend*, which depicts him as a knight from Cappadocia, whose rescue of a maiden from a dragon led to the baptism of thousands of people in Silene, Libya. He is the patron saint of England, soldiers, and Boy Scouts.

Gertrude of Nivelles. Feast day March 17; abbess; b. Landen, 626; d. Nivelles, 659. Gertrude was an example of virtue and became abbess of a monastery, which had been founded by her widowed mother, in what is now Belgium. She is often invoked against mice.

Giles. Feast day September 1; hermit and abbot; birth date and origin unknown; d. ca. 720. According to legend, King Flavius was hunting a deer that Giles was trying to protect behind a bush. When a king's huntsman wounded Giles, the king began to have a series of conversations with Giles that led to the donation of land for an abbey on the condition that Giles would be the abbot. Giles is the patron saint of beggars, lepers, cripples, and nursing mothers.

Gregory the Great. Feast day September 3; Pope, Doctor of the Church; b. Rome, February 3, 540; d. Rome, March 12, 604. Pope Gregory I often referred to himself as "the servant to the servants of God," a phrase still used by popes. His pontificate lasted from 590 to 604. He was an able politician and theologian who forged alliances and doctrines that formed the medieval Church. After having a dream of a blonde youth, he also sent missionaries to Britain. He is the patron saint of students, teachers, and musicians.

The Holy Innocents. Feast day December 28; martyrs; first century. Herod, upon learning that the one true King of the Jews had been born and after being duped by the Magi, decreed that all the male children under two be killed in Bethlehem. The Holy Innocents are the children who were killed not because of Christ but instead of him. Estimates vary, but it is believed that the number of the Holy Innocents ranges from between six and twenty-five.

Hubertus/Hubert. Feast day November 3; Bishop of Liege, b. ca. 655; d. Tervueren (near Brussels), May 30, 727. As a young man, Hubert led a worldly life. One day while hunting, he came upon a giant stag. When the stag turned toward him, there was a crucifix suspended between its antlers. The stag then talked to Hubert and told him to mend his ways or be prepared to fall into hell. Hubert is the patron saint of hunters.

Ignatius of Loyola. Feast day July 31; founder and first general of the Society of Jesus; b. Casa Torre of Loyola, Azpeitia, province of Guipúz-coa, Spain, 1491; d. Rome, July 31, 1556. Son of Basque nobility, he was a soldier until wounded at the siege of Pamplona. As he went through a long convalescence, he studied the life of Christ and the saints. This study led him to the decision to dedicate the remainder of his life to the service of God. He went on to found the Jesuit Order, which stressed the importance of education in the faith. He is the author of the influential *Spiritual Exercises*. The order has gone on to found many colleges and universities. He is the patron saint of spiritual exercises and retreats.

Isaac Jogues. Feast day October 19; Jesuit, martyr; b. Orleans, France, January 10, 1607; d. Auriesville, New York, October 18, 1646. He is a member of a group of men known as the Martyrs of North America. He led a successful mission to the Huron tribe of Quebec. He would later be martyred by the Mohawks, who took him to be a sorcerer and blamed him for causing a crop failure and an epidemic. He and his group of martyrs are the patron saints of North America.

James the Greater. Feast day July 25; apostle, martyr; b. date unknown; d. Jerusalem, 44. James was the first martyred apostle; his execution was ordered by Herod Agrippa. Legends exist that connect St. James with Santiago de Compostela in Spain. Legends from the Middle Ages claim that James either preached in Spain or that his relics were taken back to Santiago de Compostela; this made it a favorite destination for pilgrimages. Although a papal bull of Pope Leo XIII authenticated the site, there is little evidence to prove the legends outside the apocryphal *Greek Acts of James* that dates to no earlier than the eighth century. He is the patron saint of Spain, equestrians, and pharmacists.

Jerome. Feast day September 30; Church Father, scripture scholar, Doctor of the Church; b. Stridon (present-day northeast Italy), ca. 345; d. Bethlehem, Palestine, 419 or 420. Known for his ill humor and sarcastic wit, he was an extremely learned and complex man. His major contribution to the faith was the translation of scripture into Latin, or what is known as the Vulgate bible, of which he once wrote, "Now we have to translate the words of the Scriptures into deeds." He is the patron saint of scholars and librarians.

Joan of Arc. Feast day May 30; martyr, national patroness of France; b. Jeanne la Pucelle, Domremy, Lorraine, France, January 6, 1412; d. Rouen, France, May 30, 1431. She was prompted by voices of saints to save France during the Hundred Years' War. Although still a teenager, she convinced the dauphin and high churchman of the legitimacy of her calling. She led the French army to victory at Orleans. In 1430, she was captured by the Burgundians who sold her to their British allies. The British put her on trial for witchcraft, and she was burned at the stake. She is the patron saint of military personnel and the Women's Army Corps.

John. Feast day December 27; apostle, evangelist; b. Galilee, Israel, ca. 10; d. Ephesus, Greece, ca. 100. He is traditionally thought to be the author of the fourth gospel, three epistles, and the Book of Revelation. The last of these he wrote while exiled to the island of Patmos by the Romans for preaching the Good News. In recent times, a controversy has arisen as to the identity of the John sent to Patmos. Some scholars believe they are two different men, but as of yet, there is still just one saint recognized.

John Climachus. Feast day March 30; abbott, monk, hermit; b. Palestine, ca. 570; d. Mount Sinai, ca. 649. Becoming a monk after the death of his wife, he originally lived in a monastery, but then he sought a solitary life. During his solitude, he wrote the work known as the *Ladder to Paradise*. The word for "ladder" in Latin is *climacus*, and from the work, the monk received his name. The ladder in the book has thirty steps that correspond with the years of Christ's life. The book has been highly influential, especially in the Eastern churches.

John Frances Regis. Feast day June 16; Jesuit, missionary to the French Huguenots; b. Fontconverte, Diocese of Narbonne, southeastern France, January 31, 1597; d. La Louvesc (Ardèche), December 31, 1640. His missions to remote parts of France started a Catholic revival. He was especially humble and dedicated to the poor. He was known as a great orator who spoke in a simple fashion. During his life, he had the gift of healing. Another miracle attributed to him was a granary that replenished itself.

Saint John Paul II. Feast day [00 date to come]; pope; b. Wadowice, Poland, May 18, 1920; d. Vatican City, April 2, 2005. Born Karol Wojtyła, he would become the first Slavic pope and the first non-Italian pope since the Renaissance. His pontificate lasted from 1978 to 2005. Known for his personal charisma, John Paul II traveled extensively during his papacy. He is considered to have played a major role in the downfall of Communism in Eastern Europe.

Joseph. Feast day March 19; carpenter, husband of the Blessed Virgin Mary; dates unknown (first century). Perhaps described best as the foster father of Jesus, he was visited by angels twice in his dreams. As a result of the first dream, he saved Mary from public humiliation by taking her into his home, and as a result of the second dream, he took his new family to Egypt and escaped the slaughter of the Holy Innocents. He is the patron saint of workers, a happy death, fathers, Mexico, and Canada.

Juan de la Cruz (John of the Cross). Feast day December 14; founder (with St. Teresa of Avila) of the Discalced Carmelites, Doctor of the Church, poet, mystic; b. Fontiveros, Spain, June 24, 1542; d. Ubeda, Andalusia, Spain, December 14, 1591. An ally of St. Teresa of Avila in the reform movement of the Carmelite Order, he was imprisoned by a faction of opposing Carmelite monks. The conditions of his captivity were extreme. At some point near the end of his imprisonment, his jailor softened, and John was allowed a candle and writing instruments, which he used to write what is considered his best poetry. He is the patron saint of contemplatives and Spanish poets.

Jude. Feast day October 28; apostle, martyr; dates unknown (first century). He was one of the twelve apostles, but beyond this fact little is known for certain. Some traditions thought he was the author of the Epistle of Jude, but modern scholars no longer think this is probable. According to tradition, he was martyred as a missionary in Persia. He is the patron saint of lost causes or those in desperate straits.

Kateri Tekakwitha (Tekawitha). Feast day July 14; first North American Indian to be canonized; b. Ossernenon (Auriesville), New York, ca. 1656; d. Caughnawaga, Canada, April 17, 1680. Known as the "Lily of the Mohawks," she contracted smallpox as a child. Although she survived, she was left badly disfigured and nearly blind. She was baptized by a Jesuit missionary on Easter Sunday 1676, after which she walked two hundred miles to live in a Christian mission near Montreal. She was a paradigm of Christian virtue. After her death, many miracles and appearances were testified to by the Jesuit missionaries. She is the patroness of ecologists and those in exile.

Lawrence. Feast day August 10; deacon, martyr; birth date unknown; d. Rome, 258. A deacon to Pope Sixtus II, he and the pope were martyred during the persecution of Valerian. According to tradition, Lawrence had been asked to turn over the treasure of the Church to a Roman prefect. Lawrence told him the poor who belonged to the Church were its treasure. The prefect then had him grilled alive, during which Lawrence said, "Turn me over; I'm done on this side!" Although this is a great story, most scholars now believe he was beheaded. He is the patron saint of cooks, the poor, and firefighters.

Louis IX, King of France. Feast day August 25; b. Poissy, April 25, 1214; d. Tunis, August 25, 1270. Known as an ideal Christian monarch, he was especially sympathetic to the plight of the poor. He led the French army on two Crusades to the Holy Land. On the second Crusade, he contracted typhoid and died in Tunis. He is the patron saint of France.

Lucy. Feast day December 13; virgin, martyr; birth date unknown; d. Syracuse, Sicily, ca. 304. She rejected the advances of a suitor; in some accounts, she accomplished this rebuff by plucking out her eyes and offering them to him. She was then executed for being a Christian. She is the patron saint of those suffering with eye ailments.

Magnus of Füssen. Feast day September 6; apostle of the Algäu; b. ca. 699; d. Füssen, Germany, September 6, ca. 746. He established a cell at Füssen on a site that later became the monastery of Sankt Mang. With the support of King Pepin, Magnus converted the local population, cleared lands for cultivation and settlement, and opened the region to iron mining. His aid is invoked against snakes, vermin, and mice.

Margaret. Feast day July 20; virgin, martyr; dates and origin unknown. She was a popular saint of the late Middle Ages, but there is no evidence of her existence. Purportedly, she lived during the reign of Diocletian and was the daughter of a pagan priest in Antioch. She converted to Christianity when sent to nurse with a Christian woman. She was eventually sent to prison where the devil in the form of a dragon swallowed her whole. She used a crucifix that she was holding to free herself from the dragon. She is the patroness of pregnant women and those in exile.

Maria Goretti. Feast day July 6; virgin, martyr; b. Corinaldo (Ancona), Italy, October 16, 1890; d. Nettuno (Rome), Italy, July 6, 1902. She was killed in an attempted rape by a youth from her neighborhood. Maria's father, Luigi, had died when she was ten. At that time, her mother had to go to work to support the family. Each day Maria was left to care for herself and five children. Knowing that the mother would be gone, Alessandro Serenelli entered the Goretti home with a knife; when Maria refused his advances, she was stabbed repeatedly. She died the next day but not before forgiving her assailant. Many miracles are said to have happened at her tomb. She is the patron saint of teenage girls and victims of rape.

Mark. Feast day April 25; evangelist; b. Jerusalem, first century; d. Alexandria(?), ca. 74. Author of the second gospel, he knew both Peter and Paul. During Paul's Roman captivity, Mark was there to comfort him. It is thought that it was during this time in Rome that Mark wrote his gospel. Tradition holds that Mark was the first bishop of Alexandria and that he was martyred there. He is the patron saint of Venice, Egypt, notaries, basket weavers, glass workers, opticians, and cattle breeders.

Martha. Feast day July 29; dates unknown (first century). The sister of Lazarus, she appears in the gospels of Luke and John. In Luke, she is busy preparing dinner while her sister, Mary, sits with the Lord. In John, she meets Jesus to tell him that Lazarus has died, and she professes her faith in him before he raises her brother. Tradition contends that along with her sister and brother, Martha went to the south of France as a missionary. She is the patron saint of cooks, innkeepers, domestic workers, restaurants, waiters, and waitresses.

Martin de Porres. Feast day November 3; Dominican; b. Lima, Peru, December 9, 1579; d. Lima, Peru, November 4, 1639. The illegitimate son of a Spanish knight and a freed slave from Panama, his father disowned his son because his complexion favored his mother's. He entered a Dominican convent in Lima as a lay helper in return for room and board. He dedicated himself to menial tasks, caring for the poor and animals, and a life of prayer and penance. Known for his humility and profound love for others, he is the patron saint of race relations and social justice.

Mary Magdalene. Feast day July 22; witness to the Resurrection; b. Magdala, Judaea, date unknown; d. Ephesus, Rome, date unknown (first century). Jesus expelled seven demons from her, after which she became a follower. She was present at the Crucifixion and was the first witness to the Resurrection. Unlike the tradition of the Eastern Church, in the West, her story has been conflated with the sinful woman in the Gospel of Luke and Mary of Bethany, who also anointed Jesus. She is the patron saint of repentant sinners, hairdressers, and the contemplative life.

Mary of Egypt. Feast day April 2; penitent, ascetic; b. probably 344; d. ca. 421. She was a harlot from Alexandria who, upon her conversion in Jerusalem, crossed the River Jordan and lived the life of a penitent hermit for forty-seven years. After her death, her corpse was found by a monk named Father Zosimus. He was unable to dig a grave for her in the dry, hard ground until a lion appeared from the desert and dug the grave with its claws. She is the patron saint of chastity and those battling temptations of the flesh.

Matthew. Feast day September 21; apostle, author of the first gospel; dates unknown (first century). At the time he was called by Jesus to be an apostle, Matthew was a publican or tax collector. Beyond being ascribed the authorship of the gospel, little is known of his later life, and traditions vary about his death or martyrdom. He is the patron saint of alcoholics, hospitals, and ships. See also Matthias.

Matthias. Feast day February 24; martyr; dates unknown (first century). In the Acts of the Apostles, Matthias is chosen by lot to replace Judas. He was the subject of a gnostic gospel that is lost and the heretical *The Acts of Andrew and Matthias*, which includes a description of his adventures among cannibals. In some later traditions, he has been confused with St. Matthew, while other traditions maintain he was stoned to death.

Nicholas. Feast day December 6; bishop; dates unknown. No historically trustworthy evidence of his ancestry or the events of his life exists, except for the fact of his episcopate. He served as the bishop of Myra in Lycia (Turkey) during the first half of the fourth century. Some think a legend about his restoring the dowries of three poor girls gave rise to the idea of St. Nicholas as the bringer of secret presents for children; in the English-speaking countries, his name was corrupted into "Santa Claus." He is the patron saint of Russia, Greece, Sicily, and pawnbrokers.

Nicholas of Tolentino. Feast day September 10; Augustinian friar; b. Sant'Angelo in Pontano, 1245; d. Tolentino, September 10, 1305. He was named after St. Nicholas of Myra, whose shrine at Bari was visited by his parents before his birth. He is the patron of babies, mothers, animals, and the souls in purgatory.

Pachomius/Pakom. Feast day May 9; founder of Cenobitism, monastic father; b. Esneh, Egypt, ca. 290; d. Egypt, 346. Upon release from the imperial army, he converted to Christianity. When he first became a monk, he lived as a hermit, but then he began to organize a community of monks under a common rule and purpose.

Patrick. Feast day March 17; apostle of Ireland, bishop; b. Bannavem Taberniae, Roman Britain, ca. 385; d. Saul at Down, Ireland, ca. 461. Most of the best-known legends about Patrick—that he explained the Trinity using a shamrock, that he drove the snakes out of Ireland, and that he single-handedly converted Ireland to Christianity—are either false or unverifiable. What is known is that he was kidnapped by Irish pirates during his youth and forced to tend livestock. He took this event as a sign of his lax faith. After he escaped, he studied for the priesthood and had a dream in which the voice of Ireland called him back to the land of his captivity. He eventually returned as the second bishop of Ireland and concentrated on spreading the Catholic faith. He is the patron saint of Ireland and Nigeria.

Paul. Feast day June 29; apostle to the Gentiles, martyr; b. Tarsus, ca.1 or 5; d. Rome, ca. 62 or 67. Born Saul and raised as a Pharisee, he was a persecutor of Christians until undergoing a conversion experience while on his way to Damascus. He was subsequently baptized as Paul and became a Christian missionary to the Gentiles. He was later executed in Rome. He is the patron saint of authors and publishers.

Paula. Feast day January 26; widow, ascetic; b. Rome, May 5, 347; d. Bethlehem, Palestine, January 26, 404. Paula, by both birth and marriage, belonged to the Roman aristocracy. She had five children with her husband and was widowed when she was in her early thirties. She then dedicated herself to God, becoming one of the Roman widows associated with St. Jerome. She followed him to Bethlehem, funded the construction of a convent and a monastery, and was placed in charge of his care. A gifted linguist, she helped Jerome with his translations. She is the patron saint of widows.

Peter. Feast day June 29; fisherman, leader of the apostles, first pope; b. Bethsaida, Galilee; d. Rome, ca. 64. He was originally named Simon, but Jesus gave him the name Peter, meaning "rock." The role of Peter in the early Church is recorded in Acts. According to tradition, he was crucified upside down in Rome, where the main altar in St. Peter's Basilica now stands.

Pio of Pietrelcina/Padre Pio. Feast day May 25; Capuchin-Franciscan priest, stigmatic; b. Pietrelcina, Italy, May 25, 1887; d. San Giovanni Rotondo, Italy, September 23, 1968. In 1918, he was assigned to the friary at San Giovanni Rotondo, and in September of that year, he received the stigmata. He could bilocate, levitate, and read hearts, among other things. Many claim that he also emitted an odor of sanctity. Although he originally met with controversy and skepticism, he was beatified by Pope John Paul II on May 2, 1999, and canonized on June 16, 2002. He is the patron saint of adolescents and civil-defense volunteers.

Rafael the Archangel. Feast day Sept. 29. One of seven archangels, Rafael's feast day is shared with the angels Michael and Gabriel. Among his biblical achievements, he cured Tobit of his blindness and found Sarah a husband. He is the patron saint of travelers, physicians, nurses, lovers, and the blind.

Rita of Cascia. Feast day May 22; mystic; b. Roccaporena near Cascia, Umbria, Italy, 1377; d. Cascia, Italy, May 22, 1457. As a child, she wanted to become a nun, but when she came of age, she acquiesced to her parents' wishes and married. Her husband was a lout, but the union produced two sons. In their eighteenth year of marriage, her husband was murdered, and then her sons died shortly after. At that point, she tried to join a local convent but was denied for many years because she was not a virgin. In 1413, she was granted admission. She became a mystic of the Cross and bore the wound of Christ from the crown of thorns on her forehead. She is the patroness of desperate cases.

Roch/Rocco. Feast day August 16 or 17; miracle worker; b. Montpellier, France, ca. 1350; d. Angera, Lombardy, ca. 1378 or 1379. Also known as Rock, he was renowned for his ability to heal, especially victims of the plague. One legend claims that when he himself contracted the plague, he was nursed back to health by a dog. Mistaken for a spy in Montpellier, he was imprisoned and eventually executed. He is the patron saint of plague victims and sick cattle.

Rose of Lima. Feast day August 23; virgin, mystic, Dominican tertiary; b. Lima, Peru, April 20, 1586; d. Lima, Peru, August 24, 1617. She was the daughter of a conquistador and is the first canonized saint of the Americas. A mystic who practiced self-mortification, she was well-known in her lifetime. Her care for destitute children, the sick, and the elderly in Lima is pointed to as the establishment of social services in Peru. She is the patron saint of Peru, South and Central America, the West Indies, and the Philippines.

Scholastica. Feast day February 10; virgin; b. Nursia, Italy, ca. 480; d. Monte Cassino, Italy, February 10, 547. The twin sister of St. Benedict, Scholastica founded a convent at Plombaria five miles from Benedict's monastery. In their adult life, the siblings met annually in a house near the monastery. Pope Gregory the Great's account of their last meeting is retold in his *Dialogues*. In this anecdote, Scholastica asked her brother to prolong his visit so that they might talk about the joys of heaven, but because it was against his monastic rule, Benedict refused. In response, Scholastica prayed, and a violent thunderstorm developed, trapping the monk. When Benedict accused Scholastica of causing the storm, she answered, "I asked you a favor, you refused. I asked God a favor, he granted it." The two spent the night talking of heaven. She died three days later. Scholastica is the patron saint of Benedictine nuns.

Sebastian. Feast day January 20; martyr; dates and origin unknown (ca. 300). Tradition has it that he was a Roman soldier and member of the imperial guard from Milan. During the persecution of Diocletian, his Christian faith was discovered, and he was ordered to die by a firing squad of sorts. He was shot with many arrows and left for dead, but the wounds were not fatal, and he was nursed back to health by the widow of another martyr. After he was discovered again by Roman forces, he was beaten to death with a cudgel. He is the patron saint of archers, athletes, and local police.

Spyridon. Feast day December 14; bishop; b. Cypress, ca. 270; d. Cypress, ca. 348. He was a married sheep farmer, yet because of his virtuous manner, he was chosen to be the bishop of Tremithus. In one famous anecdote, he used either a pottery shard or a brick, which imploded to its basic elements of earth, water, and fire, as a means of explaining the Trinity. He is the patron saint of potters.

Stephen. Feast day December 26; deacon, protomartyr; d. Jerusalem, ca. 35. The first Christian martyr, his defense of Christianity and his death by stoning is described in Acts 6–7. He is the patron saint of deacons, and in the Middle Ages, he was often invoked against headaches.

Stephen of Hungary. Feast day September 2; first king of Hungary; b. Esztergom, Hungary, ca. 973; d. Esztergom, Hungary, August 15, 1038. He became a Christian at the age of ten when his father, Duke Geza, the ruler of Hungary, converted. Named the first king of Hungary by Pope Sylvester II in the year 1000, Stephen Christianized Hungary and turned it into a feudal state. He was known for his brutal suppression of paganism and for his great care of the poor, often distributing alms while in disguise. His tomb has been the scene of many reported miracles. He is the patron saint of kings, stonemasons, and bricklayers.

Teresa of Avila. Feast day October 15; Carmelite reformer, Doctor of the Church, mystic; b. Avila, Spain, March 28, 1515; d. Alba, October 4, 1582. Teresa of Avila is best known for her writings and mystical experiences. She believed, however, that quiet prayer was a superior experience. Throughout her life, Teresa combined being a contemplative with an active daily life. She was a prolific writer, and *The Interior Castle* is considered to be her masterpiece.

Thérèse of Lisieux. Feast day October 3; Carmelite nun; b. Alençon, France, January 2, 1873; d. Lisieux, September 30, 1897. Known as the "Little Flower," a name taken from the subtitle of her autobiography, she fulfilled her vocation and achieved sanctity "without going beyond the common order of things" (from bull of canonization, Pius XI). She is the patroness of missionaries, aviators, and florists.

Thomas. Feast day December 21; apostle, martyr; dates unknown (first century). He was one of the twelve apostles, most remembered as "Doubting Thomas" because he claimed he would not believe Christ had returned from the dead unless he could put his fingers in the wounds of the risen Lord. A rich tradition states that Thomas went on to India where he preached the Gospel and was eventually martyred. However, there is little historical evidence to support this claim. He is the patron saint of India and architects.

Thomas Aquinas. Feast day January 28; Dominican theologian, Doctor of the Church; b. Roccasecca, near Monte Cassino, ca. 1225; d. Fossanuova, near Maenza, March 7, 1274. He was an extremely prolific writer and influential thinker. If it was Augustine who "baptized" Plato, then it was Aquinas who "baptized" Aristotle. He was traveling to the Second Council of Lyon when he suffered a stroke and died soon after. He is the patron saint of booksellers (especially sellers of this book), students, and Catholic universities.

Valentine. Feast day February 14; martyr; b. date unknown (third century); d. ca. 269. There is little known of the saint. There is also some confusion if the feast day is for two Valentines: one, a priest from Rome; another, a bishop from Terni. Others believe the bishop was brought to a spot on the Flaminian Way, two miles outside of Rome to be martyred. No one knows why the saint became the patron saint of lovers either, although there is speculation that the feast day was thought of in pagan lore as the day birds chose their mates.

Venantius of Camerino. Feast day May 18; martyr; b. ca. 235; d. Camerino, Italy, ca. 252. According to legend, he was a teenager when he refused to renounce his faith, so he was tortured extensively. Venantius was scourged, burnt with torches, and suspended head down over a fire. He also had his teeth knocked out and his jaw broken. He was fed to a lion that would only lick him, and then the future saint was thrown off a cliff. When all these actions failed to kill him, he was finally martyred when he was beheaded. He is the patron saint of the city of Camerino.

Vilgefortis/Wilgefortis/Starosta. Feast day July 20; virgin, martyr; dates unknown. No historical evidence exists to validate this story in which Wilgefortis, a princess of Portugal who had taken a vow of virginity, was promised to be married to the king of Sicily by her father. The princess prayed for divine help, and as a result of her prayers, she grew a full moustache and beard. The king of Sicily withdrew his proposal. Infuriated, her father had Wilgefortis crucified. Many scholars believe the story is a product of gender confusion caused by some depictions of Christ as fully robed on the cross on certain crucifixes. She is the patron saint of abused women.

Vincent de Paul. Feast day September 27; apostle of charity, founder of the Congregation of the Mission (Vincentians) and of the Daughters of Charity; b. Pouy (now called Saint-Vincent de Paul), Landes, France, April 24, 1581; d. Paris, September 27, 1660. He equated prayer with caring for the sick and poor, so members of his order were not enclosed but of the world. He is the patron saint of charitable societies and charitable works.

Vitus. Feast day June 15; martyr; dates unknown (ca. 300?). Legend claims that Vitus was the son of a senator in Sicily. He was converted to Christianity by his tutor and his nurse. When he refused to denounce his faith, the three escaped to Rome. Once there, Vitus cured Diocletian's son of demonic possession. For his trouble, Vitus was condemned to death for sorcery by the emperor. He is often invoked against neurological diseases such as epilepsy and chorea (St. Vitus's dance). He is the patron saint of dancers, actors, and comedians.

Walter of Pontoise. Feast day April 8; abbot; b. Andainville, Picardy, ca. 1025; d. Pontoise, Normandy, 1095 or 1099. A reluctant abbot, he tried three times to escape or be relieved of his duties so that he could live a life of solitude, which he desired. His last entreaty was denied by Pope Gregory VII. One often-told anecdote of his early days as a novice in the monastery at Rebais claims he took pity on an inmate of a monastic prison; Walter not only fed the convict but helped him escape. Not surprisingly, he is the patron saint of prisoners.

Zita. Feast day April 27; virgin; b. Monsagrati, near Lucca, Italy, 1218; d. Lucca, April 27, 1278. At the age of twelve, Zita, reared religiously by poor, devout parents, entered the service of the Fatinelli family of Lucca, where she remained until her death. Her coffin, opened in 1446, 1581, and 1652, revealed her body intact. She is the patroness of domestic servants and maids.

Sources Consulted

Attwater, Donald. *The Penguin Dictionary of Saints*. Baltimore: Penguin Books, 1965.

Biography in Context. http://www.gale.cengage.com/InContext/bio.htm.

Butler, Alban. *Lives of the Saints*. Edited by Herbert Thurston and Donald Attwater. New York: Kenedy, 1963.

McBrien, Richard. *Lives of the Saints: From Mary and St. Francis of Assisi to John XXIII and Mother Teresa*. San Francisco: Harpers, 2001.

New Catholic Encyclopedia. Detroit: Gale, 2003.

Appendix II: The Poets

Kelli Russell Agodon is the author of *Hourglass Museum* (2014) and *Letters from the Emily Dickinson Room* (2010), winner of the *ForeWord* magazine Book of the Year Prize in Poetry and a finalist for the Washington State Book Award. She is also the author of *Small Knots* and the chapbook *Geography*. Agodon recently coedited the first e-book anthology of contemporary women's poetry, *Fire on Her Tongue*. Her work has appeared in magazines and journals, such as *The Atlantic*, *Prairie Schooner*, and *North American Review*, as well as on *The Writer's Almanac* with Garrison Keillor. She is the editor of Seattle's literary journal, *Crab Creek Review*, and the cofounder of Two Sylvias Press. She lives in the Northwest where she is an avid mountain biker and kayaker. Visit her website at www.agodon.com.

Ned Balbo's third book, *The Trials of Edgar Poe and Other Poems*, received the 2012 Poets' Prize and the 2010 Donald Justice Prize selected by A. E. Stallings. His previous books are *Lives of the Sleepers*, winner of the Ernest Sandeen Prize and *ForeWord* Book of the Year Gold Medal, and *Galileo's Banquet*, winner of the Towson University Prize. He is also the author of the chapbook *Something Must Happen*. Balbo has received three Maryland Arts Council grants, the Robert Frost Foundation Poetry Award, and the John Guyon Literary Nonfiction Prize. "My Father's Music," an essay on adoptive identity and ethnicity, appears in Creative Nonfiction's anthology of Italian-American prose, *Our Roots Are Deep with Passion*. He teaches at Loyola University, Maryland.

Charlotte Barr has published three volumes of poetry: *Sister–Woman* (1989), *The Bell Buckle Years* (1992), and *The Text Beneath* (2011). Her work first appeared in the *Sewanee Review*. Barr was once a member of the Dominican Sisters of Nashville. She recently retired from a long career in teaching, most recently at the Baylor School in Chattanooga, Tennessee, where she was poet-in-residence for fifteen years.

Jennifer Bates has published one full-length collection, *The First Night Out of Eden* (1998). She works for Middlebury College in various capacities, including the Bread Loaf Writer's Conference and the *New England Review*.

Joseph Bathanti is the poet laureate of North Carolina. He is the author of eight books of poetry: *Communion Partners* (1986); *The Feast of All Saints* (1994); *Anson County* (2005); *Land of Amnesia* (2009); *Restoring Sacred Art* (2010), winner of the 2010 Roanoke Chowan Prize; *This Metal* (2012), nominated for the National Book Award; *Sonnets of the Cross* (2013); and *Concertina* (2013). His novel *East Liberty* (2001) won the 2001 Carolina Novel Award. His latest novel, *Coventry* (2006), won the 2006 Novello Literary Award. His book of stories, *The High Heart* (2007), won the 2006 Spokane Prize. His collection of personal essays, *Half of What I Say Is Meaningless*, won the 2012 Will D. Campbell Award for Creative Nonfiction. He is the recipient of Literature Fellowships from the North Carolina Arts Council in 1994 (for poetry) and 2009 (for fiction); the Samuel Talmadge Ragan Award, presented annually for outstanding contributions to the fine arts of North Carolina over an extended period; the Linda Flowers Prize; the Sherwood Anderson Award; the Barbara Mandigo Kelly Peace Poetry Prize; the 2011 Donald Murray Prize; the 2012 Ragan-Rubin Award; the 2013 Mary Frances Hobson Prize; and others. Named the Gilbert-Chappell Distinguished Poet for the Western Region for the North Carolina Poetry Society for 2011–2012, Bathanti is professor of creative writing and writer-in-residence of Watauga Global Community at Appalachian State University.

Alan Berecka has published three full-length collections: *The Comic Flaw* (2009), *Remembering the Body* (2011), and *With Our Baggage* (2013). His poems have also appeared in *The American Literary Review*, *The Texas Review*, *Penwood Review*, *Ruminate*, *Windhover*, and *The Christian Century*. Some of his poems have been translated into Lithuanian and Chinese. He is a reference librarian at Del Mar College in Corpus Christi, Texas.

Kevin Brown is a professor at Lee University. He has published one full-length collection of poetry, *Exit Lines* (2009), and two chapbooks: *Abecedarium* (2011) and *Holy Days: Poems*, winner of the 2011 Split Oak Press Chapbook Contest. He also has a memoir, *Another Way: Finding Faith, Then Finding It Again* (2012), and a book of scholarship, *They Love to Tell the Stories: Five Contemporary Novelists Take on the Gospels* (2012). He received his MFA from Murray State University.

Laurie Byro was named one of the "Poets of the Decade" for 2000–2010 in the InterBoard Poetry Community competition, receiving forty Inter-Board poetry awards during this time, judged by Toi Derricotte, Mark Doty, and Ha Jin, among others. Her work has appeared in three anthologies, most recently *The Poetry of Place: An Anthology of Northern New Jersey Poets* and *Jewish Currents*. She is published widely in university presses throughout the United States, and her work has also appeared internationally in print and in many e-zines, most recently *The Paterson Literary Review*. Her children's poem "A Captain's Cat" appeared in *Cricket Magazine* and in the textbook *Measuring Up to the Illinois Learning Standards*. Byro is head of circulation at the Lee Memorial Library and poet laureate of Allendale, New Jersey. She has been happily hosting her poetry circle, Circle of Voices, for more than a dozen years.

Ann Cefola is the author of *St. Agnes, Pink-Slipped* (2011), *Sugaring* (2007), and the translation *Hence this cradle* (2007). A Witter Bynner Poetry Translation Residency recipient, she also received the Robert Penn Warren Award judged by John Ashbery. In 2013, she participated in the Pulitzer Remix (www.pulitzerremix.com), which tasked eighty-five poets from seven countries with creating poems from Pulitzer novels for National Poetry Month. Her work has appeared in anthologies, such as *Rabbit Ears: Poems about TV* (2013) and *Journey to Crone* (2013), and in journals, such as *Feminist Studies* and *Natural Bridge*. Her translations have been featured in *Absinthe*, *Action Yes*, and *Rhino*, among others. Cefola, who holds an MFA in poetry from Sarah Lawrence College, works in Midtown Manhattan as a writer and lives in the New York suburbs. To learn more, visit Cefola's literary and arts blog at www.annogram.blogspot.com.

Jim Daniels's most recent collection is *Birth Marks* (2013). Other recent books include *Trigger Man: More Tales of the Motor City* (2011), winner of the Midwest Book Award; *Having a Little Talk with Capital P Poetry* (2011), winner of the Poetry Gold Medal in the Independent Publisher Book Awards; and *All of the Above* (2011). In 2010, he wrote and produced the independent film *Mr. Pleasant*, his third produced screenplay, which appeared in more than a dozen film festivals across the country, and he wrote *From Milltown to Malltown* (a collaborative book with photographs of Homestead, Pennsylvania). His poems have been featured on Garrison Keillor's "Writer's Almanac," in Billy Collins's *Poetry 180* anthologies, and in Ted Kooser's American Life in Poetry series. His poem "Factory Love" is displayed on the roof of a race car. Daniels has received the Brittingham Prize for Poetry, the Tillie Olsen Prize, the Blue Lynx Poetry Prize, two fellowships from the National Endowment for the Arts, and two fellowships from the Pennsylvania Council on the Arts. His poems have appeared in the *Pushcart Prize* and *Best American Poetry* anthologies. He lives in Pittsburgh, where he teaches at Carnegie Mellon as the Thomas Stockham Professor of English.

Kate Daniels has published several collections of poetry, including *The Niobe Poems* (1988), *Four Testimonies* (1998), and *A Walk in Victoria's Secret* (2010). She won the Agnes Lynch Starrett Poetry Prize for *The White Wave* (1984). She also edited Muriel Rukeyser's selected poems *Out of Silence* (1992) and coedited the literary journal *Poetry East* from 1980–1990. Daniels has won the Hanes Award for Poetry from the Fellowship of Southern Writers, a Pushcart Prize, the Louisiana Literature Prize for Poetry, the James Dickey Prize, the *Crazyhorse* Prize for Poetry, and fellowships from the Lannan Foundation and Harvard University's Bunting Institute. Her work has been widely anthologized, including in *Best American Poetry*. Currently, she is a Guggenheim Fellow in poetry, but Daniels will soon return to her position as professor of English and director of creative writing at Vanderbilt University.

CX Dillhunt is the author of *Things I've Never Told Anyone* (2007) and *Girl Saints* (2003), as well as coauthor of *Double Six* (1994) with his son Drew.

He is the editor of *Hummingbird: Magazine of the Short Poem* and was coeditor of the *Wisconsin Poets' Calendar: 2006*. Nominated for a Pushcart Prize in 2013, Dillhunt was the 2012 first-place winner of the Wisconsin Book Festival Poetry Award for a series of poems titled *From the Incomplete Glass Man's Glossary*, which includes the lead poem "Window—Window Our Lady" about *Notre Dame de la Belle Verrière* at Chartres Cathedral and was published by the Wisconsin Academy of Sciences, Arts, & Letters. In the art exhibit "Haiku: Double Vision" at the Overture Center (Madison, 2006), his haiku were paired with prints, drawings, and photos by four local artists. His prose poem "On the Way to Riley" is part of the CD collection *PoetSongs: A Wisconsin Year in Poetry and Song* (music by Charyl K. Zehfus), performed at the Michael John Kohler Arts Center (Sheboygan, 2002), and his poems about teaching English in China have appeared recently in *Studio*, an online international poetry journal at York University, Toronto. Dillhunt teaches elementary school and adult writing workshops. He was named a Commended Poet by the Wisconsin Poet Laureate Commission in 2010.

Brian Doyle is the editor of *Portland Magazine* at the University of Portland. His work has appeared in the annual *Best American Essays*, *Best Spiritual Writing*, and *Best Science and Nature Writing* anthologies; among his thirteen books are the novel *Mink River*, the story collection *Bin Laden's Bald Spot*, and two books of "proems," *Thirsty for the Joy* and *Epiphanies and Elegies*.

Sandra Duguid was born and raised in rural western New York, outside Batavia. She has published one full-length collection, *Pails Scrubbed Silver* (2013). Her poetry has appeared in anthologies, such as *On Turtle's Back: An Anthology of New York State Poetry*, *The Risk of Birth*, and *A Widening Light: Poems of the Incarnation*; and in magazines, such as *Journal of New Jersey Poets*, *Modern Poetry Studies*, *America*, *Anglican Theological Review*, *Paterson Literary Review*, *Radix*, *Earth's Daughter*, and *West Branch*. She was awarded a Fellowship in Poetry from the New Jersey State Council on the Arts and was invited to read her poetry at the Geraldine R. Dodge Poetry Festival. One of her poems received Honorable Mention in the

Allen Ginsberg Poetry Contest, and another received a prize in a contest sponsored by Calvin College. She lives in New Jersey with her husband, Henry Gerstman.

Martín Espada is called the Latino poet of his generation. He has published more than fifteen books as a poet, editor, essayist, and translator. His latest collection of poems, *The Trouble Ball* (2011), is the recipient of the Milt Kessler Award and an International Latino Book Award. *The Republic of Poetry* (2006) received the Paterson Award for Sustained Literary Achievement and was a finalist for the Pulitzer Prize. The book of poems *Imagine the Angels of Bread* (1996) won an American Book Award and was a finalist for the National Book Critics Circle Award. Some of Espada's other poetry collections include *A Mayan Astronomer in Hell's Kitchen* (2000), *City of Coughing and Dead Radiators* (1993), and *Rebellion Is the Circle of a Lover's Hands* (1990). He has received numerous awards and fellowships, including the Robert Creeley Award, the National Hispanic Cultural Center Literary Award, the PEN/Revson Fellowship, and a Guggenheim Foundation Fellowship. His work has been widely translated; collections of poems have recently been published in Spain, Puerto Rico, and Chile. A former tenant lawyer, Espada is a professor in the Department of English at the University of Massachusetts Amherst.

Tyler Farrell has published two full-length collections with Salmon Poetry, Ireland: *Tethered to the Earth* (2008) and *The Land of Give and Take* (2012). He has published poems, essays, and reviews in many periodicals as well as a biographical essay for James Liddy's *Selected Poems* (2011). He currently teaches writing and literature at Marquette University and lives in Madison, Wisconsin, with his wife Joan and their two sons.

Brett Foster's first book of poetry is *The Garbage Eater* (2011), and a second collection, *Fall Run Road* (2013), was awarded Finishing Line Press's Open Chapbook Prize. His writing has appeared in *AGNI*, *Atlanta Review*, *Boston Review*, *Columbia*, *The Common*, *The Georgia Review*, *Harvard Review*, *Hudson Review*, *Image*, *Kenyon Review*, *Literary Imagination*, *Pleiades*, *Poetry Daily*, *Poetry East*, *Raritan*, *Seattle Review*, *Shenandoah*, and

Southwest Review. He teaches Renaissance literature and creative writing at Wheaton College.

Alice Friman's sixth, and most recent, collection is *The View from Saturn* (2014). Her fifth is *Vinculum* (2012), for which she won the 2012 Georgia Author of the Year Award in Poetry. She is a recipient of the 2012 Pushcart Prize and is included in *Best American Poetry 2009*. Other books include *The Book of the Rotten Daughter* and *Zoo*, which won the Sheila Margaret Motton Prize from the New England Poetry Club and the Ezra Pound Poetry Award from Truman State University. Her new work appears in *The Georgia Review*, *The Gettysburg Review*, *Image*, *Southern Review*, and others. Friman lives in Milledgeville, Georgia, where she is poet-in-residence at Georgia College. Her podcast series *Ask Alice* is sponsored by the Georgia College MFA program and can be viewed online on YouTube.

Trina Gaynon has volunteered with WriteGirl, an organization in Los Angeles providing workshops and mentors for high-school girls interested in writing. She also works with an adult literacy program. A graduate of the creative-writing program at the University of San Francisco, her poems appear in the anthologies *Bombshells* and *Knocking at the Door* as well as numerous journals, including *Natural Bridge*, *Reed*, and the final issue of *Runes*. Forthcoming publications include the chapbook *The Alphabet of Romance*, *Phoenix Rising from the Ashes: Anthology of Sonnets of the Early Third Millennium*, and *Obsession: Sestinas for the 21st Century*.

Dana Gioia has published four full-length collections of poetry, among them *Daily Horoscope* (1986) and *Pity the Beautiful* (2012), as well as many literary anthologies, including *The Longman Anthology of Short Fiction* and *Literature: An Introduction to Fiction, Poetry, Drama, and Writing*. His poems, translations, essays, and reviews have appeared in many magazines, including *The New Yorker*, *The Atlantic*, *The Washington Post Book World*, *The New York Times Book Review*, *Slate*, and *The Hudson Review*. He has written two opera libretti and is an active translator of poetry from Latin, Italian, and German. He served as chairman of the National Endowment for the Arts from 2003 to 2009. In 2011, he became the Judge Widney

Professor of Poetry and Public Culture at the University of Southern California, where he teaches each fall semester. He and his wife, Mary, have two sons. He divides his time between Los Angeles and Sonoma County, California.

Rachael Graham completed an MFA in creative writing at George Mason University in May 2012. Her poetry won two awards in the 2011 and 2012 Poetry Society of Virginia contest. Graham is also an award-winning ceramic artist, cake decorator, and playwright. She is a technical writer and editor and freelance journalist, and she lives in Fairfax, Virginia, with her husband.

Maryanne Hannan's poems have been published in *Christianity and Literature, The Other Journal, Anglican Theological Review, The Christian Century, Gargoyle, Magma, Light Quarterly, 1110, Pebble Lake Review, Poet Lore*, and numerous anthologies. She lives in upstate New York, where she taught Latin for many years.

Lois Marie Harrod recently published her thirteenth book, *Fragments from the Biography of Nemesis* (2013). She won the 2012 Tennessee Chapbook Prize for her book *The Only Is*. Her eleventh book, *Brief Term* (2011), contains poems about teaching, and her chapbook *Cosmogony* won the 2010 Hazel Lipa Chapbook contest at Iowa State University. Her chapbook *Furniture* won the 2008 Grayson Press Poetry Prize. Previous publications include the following books and chapbooks: *Firmament* (2007), *Put Your Sorry Side Out* (2005), *Spelling the World Backward* (2000), *This Is a Story You Already Know* (1999), *Part of the Deeper Sea* (1997), *Green Snake Riding* (1994), *Crazy Alice* (1991), *Every Twinge a Verdict* (1987). Retired high-school teacher and present creative-writing professor at the College of New Jersey, she won her third poetry fellowship from the New Jersey State Council on the Arts in 2003, and since 2008, she has had five fellowships at the Virginia Center for Creative Writing. More than five hundred of her poems have been published online and in print journals, including *American Poetry Review, Blueline, The MacGuffin, Salt, The Literary Review, Verse Daily*, and *Zone 3*.

Lorraine Healy, an Argentinean poet, has written *The Habit of Buenos Aires*, winner of the Patricia Bibby First Book Award (2009), as well as the chapbooks *The Farthest South*, which won First Prize from New American Press (2003); *The Archipelago* (2004); and *Abraham's Voices* (2013). She holds an MFA from New England College and a post-MFA in creative-writing teaching from Antioch University, Los Angeles. Healy has taught at the university level for years and now prefers to teach private seminars and workshops at home on Whidbey Island, Washington. She is also a fine-arts photographer who will do some commercial work, if pressed. She has been published in *Calyx*, *The Seattle Review*, *The Briar Cliff Review*, *Nimrod*, *Puerto del Sol*, and *Raven Chronicles*, among others. The poem "Saint Rita" came out of Healy's three-week journey to Italy with her mother, where they visited as many of her mother's beloved saints as they could manage in the July heat.

Edward Hirsch's first collection of poetry, *For the Sleepwalkers* (1981), received the Lavan Younger Poets Award from the Academy of American Poets and the Delmore Schwartz Memorial Award from New York University. His second collection, *Wild Gratitude* (1986), received the National Book Critics Circle Award. Since then, he has published several books of poems, most recently *Special Orders* (2008); *Lay Back the Darkness* (2003); *On Love* (1998); *Earthly Measures* (1994); and *The Night Parade* (1989). He has received fellowships from the Guggenheim and MacArthur Foundations, an Ingram Merrill Foundation Award, a National Endowment for the Arts Fellowship, the Rome Prize from the American Academy in Rome, an Academy of Arts and Letters Award, and a Lila Wallace-Reader's Digest Writers' Award. He has been professor of English at Wayne State University and the University of Houston. He is currently the president of the John Simon Guggenheim Memorial Foundation. In 2008, he was elected chancellor of the Academy of American Poets.

Mary Karr's first memoir, *The Liars' Club*, won nonfiction prizes from the PEN American Center and the Texas Institute for Letters, was a finalist for the National Book Critics Circle Award, and was a *New York Times* bestseller for more than a year. She has also received Pushcart Prizes for both verse and essays, the Whiting Award, a Guggenheim Fellowship in poetry, and Radcliffe's Bunting Fellowship. She has published four collections of poetry: *Abacus* (1987), *The Devil's Tour* (1993), *Viper Rum* (1998), and *Sinners Welcome* (2006). Her poetry appears frequently in *The New Yorker*. She is the Peck Professor of Literature at Syracuse University.

Terry Kirts is the author of *To the Refrigerator Gods*, a selection for the Editor's Choice series in poetry by Seven Kitchens Press in 2010. A senior lecturer in creative writing at Indiana University–Purdue University in Indianapolis, his poetry has appeared in *Third Coast*, *Gastronomica*, *Alimentum*, *Sycamore Review*, *Another Chicago Magazine*, and many other journals and anthologies. He is a dining critic and contributing editor at *Indianapolis Monthly* magazine.

Greg Kosmicki's books and chapbooks include *when there wasn't any war* (1987); *How Things Happen* (1997); *nobody lives here who was this sky* (1998); *For My Son in a Motel Room* (1999); *tables, chairs, wall, window* (2000); *Greg Kosmicki's Greatest Hits: 1975–2000* (2001); *The Patron Saint of Lost and Found* (2003); *Some Hero of the Past* (2006); *We Have Always Been Coming to This Morning* (2007); *Marigolds* (2009); and *New Route in the Dream* (2011). His poems have been published in numerous literary magazines, including *Paris Review*, *New York Quarterly*, *New Letters*, *Cimarron Review*, *Cortland Review*, *The Smoking Poet*, *Lily*, *ABZ*, and many others. He is the recipient of two Individual Artists Fellowships from the Nebraska Arts Council. Minnesota Public Radio's Garrison Keillor has chosen three of Kosmicki's poems to read on *The Writer's Almanac*. Kosmicki works as an adult protective services worker in Omaha, Nebraska. He is the founder and publisher of the Backwaters Press, a nonprofit literary press. He and his wife of forty years, Debbie, have three children and one grandchild. "I always had the memory of finding the Catechism after having given up hope of finding it. I really did pray to that Saint! Years later, when I was sitting around late at night searching for a subject for a poem, this popped up. I have always felt that the Patron Saint of Lost and Found saved it for me and gave it to me when I needed it."

Dean Kostos's poetry collections include *Rivering* (2012), *Last Supper of the Senses* (2005), *The Sentence That Ends with a Comma* (1999), and *Celestial Rust* (1994). He coedited *Mama's Boy: Gay Men Write about Their Mothers* (2000), a Lambda Book Award finalist, and edited *Pomegranate Seeds: An Anthology of Greek-American Poetry* (2008). His poems, translations, and personal essays have appeared in *Boulevard*, *Chelsea*, *The Cimarron Review*, *The Cincinnati Review*, *Southwest Review*, *Western Humanities Review*, on Oprah Winfrey's website Oxygen.com, and in more than 250 journals. His choral text, *Dialogue: Angel of War, Angel of Peace*, was set to music by James Bassi and performed by Voices of Ascension. He has taught at Wesleyan, the Gallatin School of New York University, and the City University of New York and has served as literary judge for Columbia University's Gold Crown Awards. A recipient of a Yaddo Fellowship, Kostos also serves on the editorial board of the *Journal of the Hellenic Diaspora*. His poem "Subway Silk" was translated into a short film by filmmaker Jill Clark.

Karen Kovacik is Indiana's poet laureate. She is author of *Metropolis Burning* (2005), *Beyond the Velvet Curtain* (1999), and *Nixon and I* (1998) as well as translator of Agnieszka Kuciak's *Distant Lands: An Anthology of Poets Who Don't Exist* (2013). Her poems, stories, and translations of Polish poetry have appeared in *APR*, *Boston Review*, *Crazyhorse*, *Colorado Review*, *Glimmer Train*, *Salmagundi*, *Southern Review*, and *West Branch*. She is the recipient of the Charity Randall Citation from the International Poetry Forum and the Barbara Mandigo Peace Poetry Prize from the Nuclear Age Peace Foundation. She also received a Fellowship in Literary Translation from the National Endowment for the Arts and a Fulbright Research Grant to Poland.

Meredith Kunsa received an MPA in public administration and an MFA in creative writing from California State University, San Diego—the city where she currently lives with her husband. Her poems have appeared in the *Connecticut Review*, *Crab Orchard Review*, *Inkwell*, *Kalliope*, *Los Angeles Review*, *Natural Bridge*, *Passager*, *Persimmon Tree*, *Raven Chronicles*, *Silk Road*, *Tiferet*, and *The Other Journal*, among others. The "St. Colman" poem was written during a month-long International Writers Program at the University of Ireland, Galway.

Gerry LaFemina is the author of a book of short stories; three collections of prose poems, most recently *Notes for the Novice Ventriloquist* (2013); and eight collections of poems, most recently *Little Heretic* (2014), *Steam Punk* (2012), and *Vanishing Horizon* (2011). His first novel, *Clamor*, was released in 2013. He directs the Frostburg Center for Creative Writing at Frostburg State University, where he is an associate professor of English. He divides his time between Maryland and New York.

Denise K. Lajimodiere is a citizen of the Turtle Mountain Band of Chippewa located in the Turtle Mountains of north-central North Dakota. She has been named an associate poet laureate of North Dakota. She has published one full-length collection, *Dragonfly Dance* (2010). Her poems have appeared in *Yellow Medicine Review*, *North Country*, and several anthologies. She holds a doctorate degree in educational administration from the University of North Dakota and is currently an assistant professor in educational leadership at North Dakota State University in Fargo. A longtime jingle dress dancer, she enjoys traveling to Pow-Wows throughout the Plains states.

Rebecca Lauren's chapbook *The Schwenkfelders* (2010) won the 2009 Keystone Chapbook Prize. Her poetry has been published in *Mid-American Review*, *Prairie Schooner*, *The Journal of Feminist Studies in Religion*, *Southeast Review*, and *The Cincinnati Review*, among others. She holds an MFA from Old Dominion University, where she won first place in the ODU–Poetry Society of Virginia–Academy of American Poets Poetry Prize Competition. A resident of Philadelphia, she teaches English at Eastern University (a Protestant institution that, unfortunately, does not believe much in saints). Lauren still occasionally drives the five hours round-trip to her hometown to have Barbara of the Barbara Shoppe cut her hair.

Jamison Lee composes poetry, fiction, and music; his work often fuses elements of each in experimental and hybrid genres. Lee's critical work addresses humor theory, digital audio poetry, writing assessment, and critical pedagogy. His most recent pieces appear in *Stanley the Whale, Cordite, Touchstone, Assessing Writing*, and NPR's *All Songs Considered*. Born and raised in Ohio, Lee is now a doctoral candidate at Illinois State University. He lives and works in Normal, Illinois.

Paul Mariani is the author of more than two hundred essays and reviews as well as of seventeen books, including seven volumes of poetry and five biographies of poets: William Carlos Williams, John Berryman, Robert Lowell, Hart Crane, and Gerard Manley Hopkins. All have been listed as Notable Books by the *New York Times*; his biography of Williams was short-listed for the American Book Award. He has also written four critical studies, including *God and the Imagination*, as well as a spiritual memoir, *Thirty Days: On Retreat with the Exercises of St. Ignatius*. He has been awarded multiple fellowships from the Guggenheim Foundation, the National Endowment for the Humanities, and the National Endowment for the Arts, and he was awarded the John Ciardi Award for Lifetime Achievement in Poetry in 2009. From 1968 until 2000, he taught at the University of Massachusetts Amherst, where he was the Distinguished University Professor of English. Since 2000, Mariani has taught at Boston College, where he holds the University Chair in English. His life of Hart Crane, *The Broken Tower*, became a feature-length film, directed by and starring James Franco; it was released in 2012 and is available on DVD, along with an interview with James Franco. Mariani's most recent book of poems is a verse autobiography, *Epitaphs for the Journey: New, Selected, and Revised Poems* (2012). His current projects include a memoir of his growing up in New York City in the 1940s and a life of Wallace Stevens for Simon and Schuster.

Erika Meitner is the author of four books of poems, including *Copia* (2014); *Makeshift Instructions for Vigilant Girls* (2011); and *Ideal Cities* (2010), which was a 2009 National Poetry Series winner. Her poems have been published in *The New Republic, Virginia Quarterly Review, APR, Tin House*, and elsewhere. She is currently an associate professor of English at Virginia Tech, where she teaches in the MFA program.

Susan L. Miller teaches poetry and expository writing at Rutgers in New Brunswick, New Jersey, and has had poems published in *Collective Brightness: LGBTIQ Poets on Religion, Faith, and Spirituality* as well as in *Meridian, Iowa Review, Commonweal, Sewanee Theological Review, Black Warrior Review, LA Review*, and other journals. She has twice received Dorothy Sargent Rosenberg Prizes for poetry. She lives in Brooklyn, New York, with her husband and daughter.

Timothy Murphy is a retired farmer and venture capitalist who hunts in the Dakotas. His most recent books are *Mortal Stakes, Faint Thunder*, and *Hunter's Log*, all published by the Lewis and Clark Fort Mandan Foundation's Dakota Institute Press in 2011.

Mary Jane Nealon has published two collections of poetry: *Rogue Apostle* (2000) and *Immaculate Fuel* (2004). Most recently, she has won Middlebury College's Bakeless Literary Award for nonfiction for her memoir *Beautiful Unbroken* (2011). Other awards include the Lucille Medwick Memorial Award from the Poetry Society of America (2001) and a grant from the New Jersey State Council on the Arts (1998).

Angela Alaimo O'Donnell teaches English and creative writing at Fordham University and serves as associate director of Fordham's Curran Center for American Catholic Studies. O'Donnell has published three full-length collections of poems, *Waking My Mother* (2013), *Saint Sinatra* (2011), and *Moving House* (2009), and two chapbooks, *Mine* (2007) and *Waiting for Ecstasy* (2009). Her work has been published in many journals, including *America, First Things, Hawaii Pacific Review, Mezzo Cammin, String Poetry, Xavier Review*, and *Valparaiso Poetry Review*, among others, and has been nominated for the Pushcart Prize, the Best of the Web Prize, and the Arlin G. Meyer Prize in Imaginative Writing. In addition to poetry, O'Donnell writes reviews and essays on contemporary literature and is a Books and Culture columnist with *America* magazine. Readers can visit her on the Web at http://angelaalaimoodonnell.com.

Jake Oresick received a BA from John Carroll University, an MS from Carnegie Mellon University, and a JD from the University of Pittsburgh. His poems have appeared in a variety of publications, including *Jones Av.*, *American Literary*, and the *Pittsburgh Post-Gazette*. An attorney and public policy consultant, he has written for *JURIST* and the *Heinz Journal*. He lives in Pittsburgh, Pennsylvania.

Melinda Palacio is an award-winning poet and novelist. She lives in Santa Barbara and New Orleans. Her poetry chapbook *Folsom Lockdown* (2009) won Kulupi Press's 2009 Sense of Place Award. She is the author of the novel *Ocotillo Dreams* (2011), for which she received the Mariposa Award for Best First Book at the 2012 International Latino Book Awards and a 2012 PEN Oakland–Josephine Miles Award for Excellence in Literature. Her short stories and poetry have appeared in various journals and anthologies. Her first full-length poetry collection, *How Fire Is a Story, Waiting* (2012) was a finalist for the Binghamton University Milt Kessler Poetry Award. Read more of Palacio's work at www.melindapalacio.com.

Suzanne Paola has published four books of poetry, most recently *Lives of the Saints* (2002). Grants and awards include a *New York Times* Notable Book Award; an American Book Award; Oprah's Bookshelf review; best book of the year listings by *Spirituality* and *Health*, *Science and Spirit*, Amazon.com, and *Library Journal*; a Pushcart Prize; a finalist for poetry's Lenore Marshall Award; and grants from the National Endowment for the Arts and other agencies. She also coauthored with Brenda Miller the nonfiction writing handbook and textbook *Tell It Slant*, which is now in its second edition. She is currently revising a new book on adoption titled *Make Me a Mother: A Memoir and Meditation of Adoption* (forthcoming from W. W. Norton) and serves with VIDA, the feminist grassroots organization representing women in the literary arts. Paola is a professor at Western Washington University, where she teaches nonfiction writing and poetry. She is also on the faculty at City University's low-residency MFA located in Hong Kong.

Jennifer Perrine's first collection of poems, *The Body Is No Machine* (2007), won the 2008 Devil's Kitchen Reading Award in Poetry. Her second book, *In the Human Zoo* (2011), received the 2010 Agha Shahid Ali Poetry Prize. She has been awarded fellowships to the Vermont Studio Center and the Kimmel Harding Nelson Center for the Arts, and she served as a member of the 2014 Arts and Culture Delegation to Cuba through Witness for Peace. Other honors include the Tor House Prize for Poetry, the *Third Coast* Poetry Prize the *Bellingham Review* 49th Parallel Poetry Award, and the Mérida Fellowship Award from US Poets in Mexico. Perrine teaches writing and gender studies at Drake University in Des Moines, Iowa.

Susan Blackwell Ramsey has published poems in *The Southern Review*, *Prairie Schooner*, *The Alaska Quarterly*, and *The Indiana Review*, among other journals. She won an Irving S. Gilmore Emerging Artist Grant in 2002, the Marjorie J. Wilson Prize from *Margie: The American Journal of Poetry* in 2006, and the Mitchell Award from the University of Notre Dame in 2008. In 2009, David Wagoner chose her "Pickled Heads" for *Best American Poetry*. Her book *A Mind Like This* (2012) won the Prairie Schooner Poetry Book Prize. She lives in Kalamazoo, Michigan.

Christine Redman-Waldeyer, founder of Adanna Literary Review, has been published in *Bird's Eye reView*, *Caduceus*, *Lips*, *Motif Magazine*, *Paterson Literary Review*, *Seventh Quarry*, *Schuykill Valley Journal*, *The Texas Review*, and *Verse Wisconsin*, among others. She has twice finaled in the Allen Ginsberg Poetry Awards. Book publications include *Frame by Frame* (2007), *Gravel* (2009), and *Eve Asks* (2011). She holds a doctorate in letters with a concentration in writing from Drew University and is currently pursuing her doctorate in education from Rowan University. She is an assistant professor of English at Passaic County Community College in Paterson, New Jersey.

Susanna Rich is an Emmy Award nominee, Fulbright Fellow in Creative Writing, and author of two Finishing Line Press chapbooks: *Television Daddy* and *The Drive Home*. She founded Wild Nights Productions, LLC, through which she tours audience-interactive poetry experiences, including *ashes, ashes: A Poet Responds to the Holocaust*; *Television Daddy*; *The Drive Home*; and *A Wild Night with Emily Dickinson*. An internationally published poet with more than 350 individual credits, Rich is professor of English at Kean University and was awarded the Presidential Excellence Award for Distinguished Teaching. She attended St. Nicholas Grammar School and Pope Pius XII High School, where she performed the lead in *The Diary of Anne Frank*. She recently completed her poetry volume *Surfing for Jesus*.

Kathleen Rooney is a founding editor of Rose Metal Press and a founding member of Poems While You Wait. She is the author of six books of poetry and nonfiction, including *Robinson Alone* (2012), winner of the 2013 Eric Hoffer Award for Poetry. Her debut novel, *O, Democracy!*, is forthcoming in 2014. She lives in Chicago.

Kristina Roth is a native of South Dakota but recently returned to California with her family and dogs after seven years in Houston. Her essays have been published in *Relief*, *Platte Valley Review*, *Blue Line*, and other literary journals. Her photographs and artwork have been published in several *Somerset* magazine titles and online at *Shutter Sisters*, *WhipUp*, and *South Dakota Magazine*. She is very excited to have rediscovered her love of bicycling.

Helen Ruggieri lives in upstate New York. Her two most recent books of poems are *Butterflies Under a Japanese Moon* (2011) and *The Kingdom Where Everybody Sings Off Key* (2013). Her poems have appeared in *Prairie Schooner*, *Hotel Amerika*, *Hawaii Pacific Review*, *Minnesota Review*, *Earth's Daughters*, *The Mom Egg*, and elsewhere. Visit www.HelenRuggieri.com for more information.

Nicholas Samaras is from Patmos, Greece, and now lives in West Nyack, New York. His first book won the Yale Series of Younger Poets Award. His next book, *American Psalm, World Psalm*, forthcoming from Ashland Poetry Press, is a study of contemporary psalms that follow modern music forms, such as American blues, jazz, folk, and world music. His work has appeared in the *New Yorker*, *Poetry*, the *New York Times*, and other national periodicals. Currently, he is the poetry editor for *The Adirondack Review*.

Mary Ann Samyn is the author of five collections of poetry: *Captivity Narrative* (1999); *Inside the Yellow Dress* (2001); *Purr* (2005); *Beauty Breaks In* (2009); and *My Life in Heaven* (2013), winner of the 2012 FIELD Prize. Her work has appeared in *Kenyon Review*, *FIELD*, *Colorado Review*, *The Journal*, *Court Green*, and elsewhere. She is a professor in the MFA program at West Virginia University.

Lauren Schmidt's poetry has been published or is forthcoming in the following journals: *The Progressive*, *Alaska Quarterly Review*, *New York Quarterly*, *Rattle*, *Nimrod*, *Fifth Wednesday Journal*, *Ekphrasis Journal*, *Wicked Alice*, and others. Her poems have been selected as finalists for the 2008 and 2009 Janet B. McCabe Poetry Prize, the Pablo Neruda Prize for Poetry, Intro to Journals Project, and the Dancing Girl Press Chapbook Contest. Her awards include the 2009 So to Speak Poetry Prize, the 2011 Neil Postman Prize for Metaphor, and the 2012 Bellevue Literary Review's Marica and Jan Vilcek Prize for Poetry. Her chapbook *The Voodoo Doll Parade* (2011) was selected as part of the 2011 Author's Choice Chapbook series, and her first collection, *Psalms of the Dining Room* (2011), is a series of poems about her experiences as a volunteer at a family-meals program in Eugene, Oregon. Schmidt now volunteers as a creative-writing teacher at a halfway house for homeless mothers in her native New Jersey. Her third book, *Two Black Eyes and a Patch of Hair Missing*, appeared in 2013.

J. D. Schraffenberger is the associate editor of the *North American Review* and an associate professor of English at the University of Northern Iowa. He is the author of the book of poems *Saint Joe's Passion* (2008), and his other work has appeared in *Apalachee Review*, *Best Creative Nonfiction*, *Brevity*, *Mid-American Review*, *Natural Bridge*, *Notre Dame Review*, *Poet Lore*, *Poetry East*, *Prairie Schooner*, *RHINO*, and elsewhere. He lives in Cedar Falls, Iowa, with his wife and two daughters.

Martha Silano has published four full-length collections: *What the Truth Tastes Like* (1999); *Blue Positive* (2006); *The Little Office of the Immaculate Conception* (2011), winner of the 2010 Saturnalia Books Poetry Prize and an Academy of American Poets Noted Book of 2011; and *Reckless Lovely* (2014). Her poems have appeared in *Paris Review*, *North American Review*, *Kenyon Review Online*, *American Poetry Review*, and *Best American Poetry 2009*, among others. Silano teaches at Bellevue College.

Alessandra Simmons is a poet, editor, and educator from Los Angeles. She earned her MFA in creative writing, poetry, from Indiana University. While at IU, she served as editor of *Indiana Review* and was a visiting lecturer at IU South Bend. Her poems have appeared (or will soon appear) in *The Other Journal*, *WomenArts Quarterly*, *Post Road*, and *Ghost Town*, among other journals. She lives in Chicago with her husband.

Sarah J. Sloat is the author of four chapbooks: *In the Voice of a Minor Saint* (2009), *Excuse me while I wring this long swim out of my hair* (2011), *Homebodies* (2012), and *Inksuite* (2013). Her poems have appeared in many print and online journals, including *Court Green*, *Hayden's Ferry Review*, *Linebreak*, and *Bateau*. She has lived in China, Kansas, Italy, and Pennsylvania. For the last couple decades, Sloat has resided in Frankfurt, Germany, where she works in news.

Erin Elizabeth Smith is the author of two full-length poetry collections: *The Fear of Being Found* (2008) and *The Naming of Strays* (2011). Her poetry has appeared in *32 Poems*, *The Yalobusha Review*, *Mid-American*, *Third Coast*, *Crab Orchard*, and *Willow Springs*, among others. She is a lecturer in the English Department at the University of Tennessee and is the founder and managing editor of Sundress Publications and the *Best of the Net Anthology*.

Annette Spaulding-Convy's full-length collection *In Broken Latin* (2012) was a finalist for the Miller Williams Poetry Prize. Her chapbook *In the Convent We Become Clouds* won the 2006 Floating Bridge Press Chapbook Award and was nominated for a Pushcart Prize. Her poems have appeared in *Prairie Schooner*, *North American Review*, and the *International Feminist Journal of Politics*, among others. She is coeditor of the *Crab Creek Review* and cofounder of *Two Sylvias Press*, which has published the first e-book anthology of contemporary women's poetry, *Fire on Her Tongue*.

James Tate's first collection of poems, *The Lost Pilot* (1967), was selected by Dudley Fitts for the Yale Series of Younger Poets while Tate was still a student at the University of Iowa Writer's Workshop, making him one of the youngest poets to receive the honor. He published prolifically over the next two decades, including *The Oblivion Ha-Ha* (1970); *Hints to Pilgrims* (1971); *Absences* (1972); *Viper Jazz* (1976); *Constant Defender* (1983); *Distance from Loved Ones* (1990); and *Selected Poems* (1991), which won the Pulitzer Prize and the William Carlos Williams Award. Most recently, he has published *The Eternal Ones of the Dream: Selected Poems 1990–2010* (2011); *The Ghost Soldiers* (2008); *Return to the City of White Donkeys* (2004); *Memoir of the Hawk* (2001); *Shroud of the Gnome* (1997); and *Worshipful Company of Fletchers* (1994), which won the National Book Award. His honors include a National Institute of Arts and Letters Award for Poetry, the Wallace Stevens Award, a 1995 Tanning Prize, and fellowships from the Guggenheim Foundation and the National Endowment for the Arts. In 2001, he was elected a chancellor of the Academy of American Poets. He teaches at the University of Massachusetts Amherst.

Maria Terrone is the author of two poetry collections: *A Secret Room in Fall* (2006), cowinner of the McGovern Prize from Ashland Poetry Press, and *The Bodies We Were Loaned* (2002). She has also written a chapbook titled *American Gothic, Take 2*. She is the recipient of first-place prizes from *Passages North*, *Wind*, and *Willow Review* magazines as well as the Arts & Culture Award from the Italian-American Labor Council. Her work, which has been published in French and Farsi, has appeared in magazines, including *Ploughshares*, the *Hudson Review*, *Poetry*, and *Poetry International*, and in twenty anthologies. In spring 2012, she was commissioned by the Guggenheim Museum to write a lyrical narrative for its "stillspotting nyc" project in Queens, which was performed over four weekends.

Victoria Edwards Tester is the winner of the Academy of American Poets Brazos Bookstore Prize and the Donald Barthelme Memorial Fellowship for Poetry. She lives near Silver City, New Mexico. *Miracles of Sainted Earth* (2002) is the first in the Mary Burritt Christiansen Poetry series published by University of New Mexico Press.

Judith Valente is an on-air correspondent for the national PBS-TV program *Religion & Ethics NewsWeekly* and a former staff reporter for the *Wall Street Journal* and the *Washington Post*. She is the author of the poetry collection *Discovering Moons* (2009) and the chapbook *Inventing an Alphabet* (2004), selected by Mary Oliver for the 2004 Aldrich Poetry Prize. She is coeditor with Charles Reynard of *Twenty Poems to Nourish Your Soul* (2005), an anthology of poems and reflections on finding the sacred in the ordinary. In 2013 she published *Atchison Blue: A Search for Silence, a Spiritual Home, and an Authentic Faith*, her memoir of her regular visits to Mount St. Scholastica Monastery in Atchison, Kansas, and *The Art of Pausing: Brief Meditations for the Overworked and Overwhelmed*, a book of haiku and meditations. She lives in Chicago and Normal, Illinois.

Wendy Vardaman has a PhD in English from the University of Pennsylvania. Coeditor and webmaster of *Verse Wisconsin* and cofounder, editor and webmaster of Cowfeather Press, her poems, reviews, essays, and interviews have appeared online and in various anthologies and journals, including *Verse Wisconsin*, *Poetry Daily*, Poets.org, *Breathe: 101 Contemporary Odes*, *Riffing on Strings: Creative Writing Inspired by String Theory*, *Poet Lore*, *qarrtsiluni*, *Antiphon*, *Mezzo Cammin*, *Women's Review of Books*, *Rain Taxi Review*, and *Portland Review*. She is coeditor of the 2013 *Wisconsin Poets' Calendar* and *Echolations: Poets Map Madison* (2013). The author of *Obstructed View* (2009), she has been nominated for numerous Pushcart Prizes and a Best of the Net Award. Vardaman has been recognized by the Council for Wisconsin Writers' awards in poetry and short nonfiction. One of two poets laureate of Madison (2012–2015), she has three children with husband Thomas A. DuBois and has never owned a car.

Susan Settlemyre Williams is the author of *Ashes in Midair* (2008), winner of the 2008 Many Mountains Moving Poetry Book Contest, and a chapbook titled *Possession* (2007). Her poetry has appeared in *Prairie Schooner*, *Mississippi Review*, *Diode*, and *Shenandoah*, among other journals, as well as in various anthologies, including, most recently, *The Ecopoetry Anthology*. She is retired from the practice of law and currently serves as literary editor and book-review editor for the online journal *Blackbird*. She lives in Richmond, Virginia.

Eliot Khalil Wilson is the author of *The Saint of Letting Small Fish Go* (2003). He has received a fellowship from the National Endowment for the Arts, a Pushcart Prize, a Bush Foundation Fellowship, the Hill-Kohn Prize from the Academy of American Poets, and the Robert Winner Prize from the Poetry Society of America. He currently teaches at the University of Colorado, Denver.

Franz Wright was born in Vienna in 1953 and grew up in the Northwest, the Midwest, and northern California. His most recent works include *Ill Lit: Selected and New Poems* (1998); *The Beforelife* (2001), a finalist for the Pulitzer Prize; and *Walking to Martha's Vineyard* (2003), which won the Pulitzer Prize for poetry. He has been the recipient of two National Endowment for the Arts grants, a Guggenheim Fellowship, a Whiting Fellowship, and the PEN/Voelcker Prize, among other honors. He lives in Waltham, Massachusetts, with his wife, the translator and writer Elizabeth Oehlkers Wright.

C. Dale Young practices medicine full-time, serves as poetry editor of the *New England Review*, and teaches in the Warren Wilson College MFA program for writers. He is the author of *The Day Underneath the Day* (2001), *The Second Person* (2007), and *Torn* (2011). A recipient of fellowships from the National Endowment for the Arts, the John Simon Guggenheim Memorial Foundation, and the Rockefeller Foundation, he lives in San Francisco.

Maged Zaher is the author of *Thank You for the Window Office* (2012), *The Revolution Happened and You Didn't Call Me* (2012), and *Portrait of the Poet as an Engineer* (2009). His collaborative work with the Australian poet Pam Brown, *Farout Library Software*, was published by Tinfish Press in 2007. His translations of contemporary Egyptian poetry have appeared in *Jacket* magazine and *Banipal*. He has performed his work at Subtext, Bumbershoot, the Kootenay School of Writing, St. Mark's Project, Evergreen State College, and the American University in Cairo, among other places. Maged lives in Seattle and works in software.

Index of Poets

Mary Ann Buddenberg Miller is a professor of English at Caldwell College in Caldwell, New Jersey, a small liberal arts college in the Dominican tradition. She received her bachelor's and master's degrees in English from the University of Dallas in Irving, Texas, and her doctorate in English literature from the Catholic University of America. She frequently teaches Masterpieces of Western Literature, Literature of the Victorian Age, Catholic Writers, Introduction to Poetry, and College Writing. Her research interests are located at the intersection of theology and literature. Her outreach efforts include offering students in the Introduction to Poetry course the opportunity to host public readings for local, published poets.

Founded in 1865, Ave Maria Press,
a ministry of the Congregation of
Holy Cross, is a Catholic publishing
company that serves the spiritual and
formative needs of the Church and its
schools, institutions, and ministers;
Christian individuals and families; and
others seeking spiritual nourishment.

For a complete listing of titles from

Ave Maria Press

Sorin Books

Forest of Peace

Christian Classics

visit www.avemariapress.com

ave maria press® / Notre Dame, IN 46556
A Ministry of the United States Province of Holy Cross